ENNEAGRAM

What You Need to Know About the Loyalist

(A Complete Self-discovery Guide to Spiritual Growth)

Jeanette Sanford

Published By **Jeanette Sanford**

Jeanette Sanford

Enneagram: What You Need to Know About the Loyalist (A Complete Self-discovery Guide to Spiritual Growth)

ISBN 978-1-77485-439-6

Legal & Disclaimer

The information contained in this book is not designed to replace or take the place of any form of medicine or professional medical advice. The information in this book has been provided for educational and entertainment purposes only.

The information contained in this book has been compiled from sources deemed reliable, and it is accurate to the best of the Author's knowledge; however, the Author cannot guarantee its accuracy and validity and cannot be held liable for any errors or omissions. Changes are periodically made to this book. You must consult your doctor or get professional medical advice before using any of the suggested remedies, techniques, or information in this book.

TABLE OF CONTENTS

Introduction

The enneagram can help you discover your personality type. The enneagram can be described as a sophisticated method that has been used for hundreds and years. The results of the enneagram are reliable and irrefutable. There are nine personality kinds within yourself. These personalities manifest in different ways. You will experience each of the nine personality types, although the dominant one is your most important. You will feel them in subtler ways. Depending upon the circumstances, you may experience a more prominent expression of some traits. These traits might align with a personality type other than yours.

Knowing your personality type can be a key step in your self-awareness journey. What you learn will open up many new perspectives about your life. Many people don't recognize their insecurities. This is why they try to hide them from others or blame them when they can't.

This book will take you through each personality type so that you are familiar with what to expect. These are the general characteristics that each personality type shares. These are not necessarily indicative of a personality type, but they can help you to get started. These types are useful as a starting point. Each personality type is further classified to show how your behavior may manifest in various ways.

This will allow you to see your feelings and actions from a fundamental viewpoint. Because it is difficult to understand the feelings and thoughts we don't have an explanation for, it can be easier to withdraw or face your fears than to acknowledge them.

We discover as we study the different personality types that everyone has something insecure. Accepting that fact is the first step to conquering your fears. Knowing what you are dealing with, its causes, and the effects on you is the first step to changing it. Insecurities are what keep us trapped in cells made of our own creation. We fear that confronting them would be unpleasant. Because no one likes to suffer, ignorance is the most common way people choose for dealing with their insecurities.

Another way is to project. Projection is another way to overcome your fears. These challenges can be overcome by understanding your personality type. You will be more confident than you realize. There are so many opportunities that you miss because of your vulnerability. Knowing the enneagram will help to guide you in your quest to self-inquiry.

You must learn to accept yourself exactly as you are. Your imperfections are perfectly normal. You are the most perfect version of yourself that you will ever see, so embrace it and be happy. You can accept yourself and live a fulfilling lifestyle. You can also use the wisdom of the enneagram to help you understand and shape your beliefs and the world around. Everyone deserves a healthy life. It is not always easy to attain, but it can be done. Your potential can only be realized if your personality type is known and used in a positive way to relate with others.

Begin your journey of self discovery by allowing yourself sufficient time to learn, without feeling pressure. The opportunities that lie ahead are more than you might imagine. Start the process and you will enjoy a fulfilling, spiritually rewarding, and satisfied life.

Chapter 1: The Enneagram And Its Historical Background

There is an old saying that "everything that has a start has an end" and vice versa. Every process begins at a point. And every bit of history is felt into the future. Enneagram follows the same pattern. Enneagram is a term that refers to its history and development. How did Enneagram develop? What caused its development? How was Enneagram invented?

Enneagram is a combination of two Greek words. Ennea means "nine" while gramma means "written." Scholars disagree on the origin of Enneagram. It was necessary because many people believed that the personalities they identified were true to form. Palmer and Wiltse opine that the book Evagrius Ponicus, a 4th-century work on the Enneagram is the first. Ponticus defined eight personalities (logismoi) as "deadly ideas" and referred to the critical thought as "love oneself". Ponticus believed this was because one's personality influences what one does when judging another person's trait.

Therefore, people with a 'challenger' personality will take enthusiasm to be a negative trait simply for not displaying it. Ponticus states further that Ponticus believes this to be true.

"Philautia, the first thought of all, is that self-love (Philautia); afterwards [come] on the eight."

Ponticus made these identifications and caused a lot commotion. People wondered how it was possible for love to be equated with personalities. How could love come into being if it weren't also altered? Ponticus offered the "remedies", which were the remedies to the eight thoughts. These solutions will answer all questions that could arise on the eight thoughts. These remedies made it clear that many people felt the need to take the Ponticus ideas seriously. Debatable is the validity of the eight thoughts as they are relevant in today's world.

However, these eight thoughts didn't get enough publicity. G.I. Gurdjieff helped make the Enneagram known all over. This could be the origin of Enneagram as it is today. It is noteworthy to point out that Gurdjieff maintained the eight Ponticus-inspired thoughts. They actually served as the guiding principles in his work.

Oscar Ichazo from Bolivia could be called the Enneagram 'inventor' today. Oscar in the 1950s gave nine personality studies that are still relevant today. These include those that emphasize ego-fixations (virtues, passions, holy ideas), and others that deal with ego. Another report claims Oscar's extensive self-development process and orientation are what led to the creation of Enneagram. Lessons in 'Proto-analysis' use the nine enneagram characters and ideas that are still used today.

Enneagram gained more attention through Oscar's teachings. The Africa institute, which is based in Chile, was created. When

Oscar moved from South America to the United States of America, however, it was later relocated. This is where the etymology of "Enneagram of Personality" can be traced. Oscar invented the term. Oscar wanted to help his students learn how to become enneagram personalities across the globe.

Claudio Naranjo was one of the first psychologists to go to Oscar to learn the Enneagram concept in the 1970s. This is why they were among the first Oscar students who understood Enneagram. Claudio Naranjo was a Chilean psychiatrist who came to Africa Institute from Arica, Chile. Naranjo was inspired by Oscar's teachings and decided to bring his Enneagram classes to the United States.

Oscar taught him that he had a different opinion about the teachings. A Jesuit priest, who was also influenced by him, adopted his teachings to spiritual dealings. Oscar did not like Enneagram's other approach. Oscar regarded Enneagram's approach as unorthodox and friendly, even though it was straightforward and friendly. Oscar disowned Naranjo because he considered his teachings to be treacherous. This despite the fact his lessons from other teachers had spread like wildfire in 70s. Naranjo was teaching Enneagram and his theory quickly grew, with students as well.

Naranjo, who also saw his teacher suffer the same fate as his students in the end, misunderstanding and even betraying him, is true to the saying, "You shall reap what your sow." Naranjo taught things that were meant to be spiritual, while his students taught things more business-oriented. Instead of preaching their teacher's teachings, they focused instead on a paradigm shifting that saw them explore and implement the business side Enneagram.

In the 1980s, Don Richard Riso, Helen Palmer, Richard Rohr (Elizabeth Wagele), Richard Rohr (and others) began various publications on Enneagram. They taught theories that were influenced by the history of Enneagram and published them. Only the context of an enneagram theory's application today can determine their usage and understanding. This book does not have any special views other than to simplify Enneagram.

Perhaps Enneagram founders understood Enneagram differently and were able to teach it in that way, leading to many Enneagram theories focusing on spirituality as well as business. Many people today want to associate Enneagram with spirituality. This is wrong considering the Enneagram's history. This account was confirmed by different authors, looking at it differently. Enneagrams are used in psychology and neuroscience. It is a recent discovery that has drawn a lot of attention.

It is worth noting that Enneagram's historical background follows a complicated pattern. The Enneagram idea has experienced rapid development from one scholar and another. Additionally, the Enneagram is constantly evolving and being developed with new ideas from young minds. Next chapter will discuss how the Enneagram concept was created.

Where Enneagram was invented

Since its inception in 4th century AD, the exact origin of Enneagram is a mystery. As we have already mentioned, Enneagram context understanding has been developed by various theories and teachings from different scholars. Many people who published works to influence others about Enneagram's meaning never intended to do so. Enneagram is one of many concepts in psychology that have been misunderstood.

Many who begin Enneagram may have some diluted knowledge of the origins. Many Enneagram theories have contributed significantly to the way we know it today. These are the most famous Enneagram places throughout history. They are where Enneagram's best understanding and discovery can be made. They are the teachings and insights of the notable, more profound Enneagram personality.

Enneagram has seen many approaches to its development and alarming concern from many professions. These include psychology, neurology, theology and many others. It is important to understand how and where it was created. It is worth noting that Enneagram personality originated from the Enneagram's diverse scholars. There is no concrete building like a pyramid or monument center.

Enneagrams' development is also based upon the fact that there exist different schools or thoughts with different terminologies. There are also approaches to conception, overlapping, merging teachings, and dealings. Even though it's quite different from its original intention today, the Enneagram you see today was created from the places it originated.

Psychologists have identified six main 'places' from which the Enneagram came to be. This is not the Enneagram's historical history. Its origins and the locations it was built are intended to simplify the teachings. Below are six locations where Enneagram is found:

Don Richard Riso

Don Richard Riso takes a neurotic approach towards the study and application of the Enneagram. Its approach is to provide a complete description of the sequence of events in each of the nine personalities. This Enneagram style was created to analyze how emotional health evolved by using the neurons within the body. Many teachings and beliefs have been developed based on this Enneagram personality type. This helps you to understand how your Enneagram personality developed.

Oscar Ichazo - Development of enneagram personalities

Ichazo is an approach that uses the nine personalities. It allows for the analysis of self development and the application using different schemata, such as fixations and ego. This approach is used in many books. This approach uses the Enneagram to guide self-development by using the fixations theories.

Hameed A. Ali - development of Enneagram personalities

Hameed A. Ali's Enneagram personalities were developed by a psychological method that evolved into another form of Enneagram. Enneagrams of personality are a combination between disciplines such as Zen and Reichian therapy, and include studies of the psychology of Gestalt. It is solely psychological. Therefore, it studies the mind and how they impact human behavior. This type of Enneagram was probably the most popular.

Claudio Naranjo's development of enneagram personality

Claudio was a psychiatrist and suggested a strategy that replaced neurotic terms and strategies using psychiatric vocabulary and dealings. The Enneagram's dependence on transactions and neurotic usage as a determinant was denied and changed. The psychiatric approach was at the heart of everything. This is because this approach is almost synonymous to human disorders. Many people do not like this approach, but those in the field are happy to use it. You should pay special attention to the terminologies in any book on Enneagram that discusses this type of personality.

Helen Palmer

Helen Palmer is an Enneagram that focuses primarily on the narrative of all the teachings. Similar to the book, this development is about learning the broad idea. Final note: This Enneagram was developed from the teachings and strategies it has used since its inception. However, Enneagram still relies on the nine human personalities as they relate to and react to other things and people. These facts lead to the conclusion that Enneagram was originally developed by a developer.

Oscar Ichazo development Enneagram personalities

The Oscar Ichazo method was developed to help you apply the nine personalities using varying schemata. Psychologists and other Enneagram developers have all agreed that those Enneagram personalities are human since birth. Noting that no new insights were found when they traced Enneagram's source to inhuman sources, The only thing that was discovered was the naming of, description, as well as teachings of the Enneagram personalities. The future of Enneagram development is in flux, so there is a good chance that we will have many more.

Last, let's not forget that Enneagram developed from several different approaches. However none of them have ruled the birth context out of Enneagram's conception. This is why Enneagram people have many misconceptions. This is the fundamental reason why Enneagram can be described as a model system and also a system that consists of nine human personalities. It uses the most commonly used names and does not perpetuate the common misconception.

This chapter should provide you with an overview of the Enneagram's various schools. Knowing the history of the concept would help you to navigate this journey. This chapter will help expand your perspective on this concept. Is there an Enneagram school you like? Which do your interests lie? All the rest will fall in place once this foundation is laid.

Chapter 2: The basics

Synopsis

Go to the website below to determine which enneagram you are.

Your dominant personality type is the most significant part of you.

The Start Point

Fill in your personality. This is a way to show what you have done over a certain period of time.

It is possible to make the worst mistake when performing this test. It can result in inaccurate findings and marred results. To make this test work correctly, you should answer every question honestly.

It is possible to choose between assertiveness, or shyness. One may desire to become more assertive but it's important to be honest with oneself about where you are in life. Your true nature is to be exactly where you are at the moment.

Once you know who you are, you will be able to see a computer generated report which will reveal 3 things.

- Your dominant type

Your wing

- Your instinctual, sub-type

These can be recorded, along with any 2nd or 3rd results. A script can often give you the results that most closely match your personality. Take the time to review the results of the 2nd or 3rd probability.

If you are a type 5 (investigator/observer), it means that you are born into that type. You've been the same type all your adult life.

Although it is possible to be content with one's growth, this doesn't mean your type changes. Instead, it simply means that someone has transformed from an unhealthy type into one that is more healthy. Keep in mind that there is no superior type. You are simply growing.

Each type has its own set strengths and weaknesses that will guide them through their entire life.

A set of core motivators is common to all types. The following can be summarized:
- Ego Fixation
- Holy Idea
- Basic Fear
- Core desire
- Biggest Temptation
- The Greatest vice
Virtue
Each individual is unique. While 2 people of the dominant type may have different exterior appearances and functions, their core desire is the exact same.

Chapter 3: The Enneagram: The Definition And Use

Enneagram has a strange sounding name. It sounds like it could be used to denote something very unusual. However, it is not a term for a disease or an electronic device attached to your brain. Either it does not refer or imply an exotic animal found in a distant place. The Enneagram is a term that refers to an unusual phenomenon that has been popularized over the last decade. It's important to remember that this chapter will expose you to many new terms. Let's go!

The Enneagram of Personality (or simply the Enneagram) is sometimes referred to by some people. However, they all know that these concepts are fundamentally identical.

Chapter 2 will give you an in-depth explanation of the personality types and provide details about their individual characteristics. The Enneagram works everywhere. No matter where you live or travel, it can be used in the exact same way and for exactly the same purpose. The Enneagram can be used anywhere, including India, Peru, America, and even the United States. Even then, being able to identify yourself could be very helpful!

The Enneagram, when used correctly can help individuals improve their emotions, better understand their history, and make better decisions about their future. Many professionals have taken the Enneagram to help patients and clients, such as psychologists, chief executive officers (CEOs), and entrepreneurs. However, it is not necessary to work in those areas to use and understand the Enneagram. This tool can really help you reach your potential, as well as enlightening you on how you can move forward in your journey to self-discovery.

Before diving into the depths of the subject and introducing each diagram per se, let us talk about what we know so far about the Enneagram. Many people are grateful to have discovered this tool because they can individually assess their personality profile and build from there-- so there's no need for expensive therapy consultations or costly seminars.Self-tests with specific instructions will help you to identity your personality type, and will be key to the next steps towards your self-transformation.In this book, I will also suggest you to use a very-well know and reliable test created by David Daniels and Helen Palmer.Both are co-authors of a bestseller regarding the Enneagram, a concept which they have studied, taught, and written about extensively.David Daniels and Helen Palmer have taken the Enneagram concept to another level by exposing as many people as possible to their discovery and beliefs.I will also list a few others tests available to you online for free in the following chapters.

Knowing and understanding your personality type can help you positively impact the relationships around you. This will make it easy to influence people in your life -- family members, friends and neighbors.

You can see the 9 personality types in the diagram. The diagram shows you that the personality types don't have to be identical. However, they interact with one another and can mix together. For example, take the personality type number 9. It is closely associated with both number 1 and number 8. This means that your identification with one personality type may not be as straightforward as black and white. You are likely to share some traits with a few, which is fine. But, there should be one personality type that stands out. It will be your Basic personality.

As you know, your primary or dominant personality should reflect the personality type that was displayed as a child. Your basic personality type applies to both men and women, regardless of how much you change. It is true that, although certain basic personality characteristics might seem to fit you perfectly, not all of them do. Each dominant personality is unique and has its own strengths and weaknesses.

Chapter 4: Understanding Personality Types

People are unique in their physical appearances. You could group them together and give names to those who share these characteristics, as we did with blonds or blacks, whites, and tall.

As we do with people's physical attributes, we can also use them to classify their personalities and their individual traits. There is a reason why things are the way they are. We have to do certain things in order to achieve success in life. Personalities are what determine who you are. They influence how you respond to different stimuli. This can alter our attitudes and reactions to certain situations.

Personalities refers to who we are as people, or more accurately the personality type we have. It affects our relationships with one another. Imagine a person who is covered in tattoos and has dreadlocks. One person might think that they are immoral people with little respect for religion, and thus dangerous. Someone else may see it as attractive and creative. These responses are a result of our personalities. This principle can be applied to our relationships. Normally, people who are unlike each other attract and end in amazing relationships. This is why people often say that "opposites attract". Imagine a world in which no one is different or unique. Your beliefs are the same as the beliefs of the next person, the other and the third. This would make you bored to your core, if you listen to the identical songs, like the exact same things, have the similar careers, have the exact same opinions, etc. While it may sound interesting and enjoyable at first, once you start to see the context and consider it all in context, it becomes monotonous and overwhelming over time. Then it would be impossible to communicate with each other because there are no new ideologies being exchanged. This would result in a loss of relationships and an absence of excitement for exploring different perspectives. This would cause no purpose or fulfillment. It would also mean that there is no reciprocity, meaninglessness, and therefore no meaning.

The other area that will be affected is our careers. We are all influenced by the same stimuli which push us into wanting the same things. However, stagnation can occur as there are so much areas that need tapped into. All of us have a purpose to live our lives. This is what makes chefs, bankers, entrepreneurs and politicians so successful.

We are pushed and motivated by different stimuli. This leads us to our intended paths. But we also are pushed differently to get to the top of our chosen paths. That is why some people go on to manage others, some become stagnant, some start rival companies, and some decide to change their lives and pursue other paths. Our personalities determine our thinking, beliefs, perceptions, and behavior. They shape who we are. They make life beautiful.

There are many different types of personalities. They are all grouped together by their strongest traits, or the most striking thing about them. We will examine each of the Nine groups and discuss how it affects their relationships, success, purpose, overall approach, and general outlook on life.

Type 1 The Perfectionist

Perfectionists are those who strive to be 100 percent. They strive to be the best in everything they do. Type Ones don't have any middle ground. They are trustworthy, reliable and use common-sense. What this means is that they will go to great lengths to improve the surroundings. No matter what seems odd, they'll go the extra mile to bring it back to where it belongs, even if it is just a slight change.

It is difficult to see things from their perspective. They feel a lack of control over their lives and are unable to see the bigger picture.

For example, they might attempt to make their partners see the world in the same way they do. This could lead them to try to find a common understanding with them about everything. In most cases, this would lead them to be proud and may make them seem rude or arrogant. This could lead them to having poor relationships. The ability to openly receive and take information from others is the key to communication and relationships. Strong beliefs can make it difficult to communicate with others.

They can also experience a variety of personality effects that affect their purpose in life. This is because they don't accept less than perfect things and are unable to take other peoples' opinions into account. They may waste time, money, energy and effort trying to prove factual errors that are not there. They might end up trying to find dead causes.

It's not all bad. Their perfectionist nature works in their favor at times. They are honest and reliable, and they try to correct mistakes and raise standards for others. They take full accountability for their actions. They are trustworthy people to consult because they see the truth for what it really is. Clarity is key in life. They have a clear vision of their journey which allows them to identify the best and worst. This is an essential tool in life. We all want to improve and work on our flaws. However, we also need to let go of the things that don't work to achieve the results we desire.

Type 2: A Giver

The Giver is the second personality. They can be described as the "fit-in crew", because they enjoy seeking approval from people they meet. Approval is very important to them. This can mean that they will make sacrifices on some other things in life. This personality is careful of what they say. They can be good people to nurture and guide. It comes at a cost, however. Being a good listener can lead to you losing your identity. The givers are very compassionate and care about everyone, including their friends and families. And while this is a wonderful trait, they can sometimes get trapped in situations where they think everyone is selfish. However they had to learn to be more selfish.

This is a positive influence on many aspects of their life, including their relationships, friendships, work and even their love life. They are extremely loving and understanding people. The fact that they take the time to get to know you and make you feel comfortable is a sign that they are a good person to have in your life. It is a pleasure to have them as friends and to work with. As I mentioned before, they can become dependent on the approval of others. A lack of approval can lead to them going through a crisis and losing their self-esteem. It can also lower their confidence in what it is they offer or bring to the table.

Independence of thought and having a cause and goal gives an individual purpose and drives. An individual lacking independence will be more susceptible to being influenced or gullible, which can lead to a narrower outlook on life and the people around him. Some might argue that Givers' adaptive, accommodating nature makes them more likeable. They are more likely to get promoted faster than others because they are more open to new opportunities. They are able to openly listen to other people's thoughts and ideas which leads to them being viewed as the go-to person. Givers can solve any problem. Their socializing skills allow them to create networks faster than others, which makes them more effective at many tasks.

A giver could be dependent on success and happiness from others, which might make him vulnerable to being taken advantage or approved by them. They might be too naive to realize they are winning trust and approval from others. In reality, they may be used for their own advantage. There is often a lot to this and, because the personality of the giver changes according to the situation it creates, they might not be appreciated for their true self. Givers love giving and are easy to get along. You have to be careful about being too nice because people can take it as theirs!

Type 3 - The Performer

The Performer personality is the third. He or she can achieve great success because he/she is goal-oriented and very motivated. They only have one goal in life: To make it big. They often put their success before their feelings or opinions. To them, the best way to present themselves is as a victim. They are so obsessed by their image that they don't have the time or energy to enjoy other aspects of life.

They are successful because they have spent a lot of their lives and time perfecting their craft. This can lead to depression, fatigue, and other psychological problems. This could be because they focus less on their physical and mental health and more on their career goals. Perfectionist and performer have certain common traits. These include their obsession with achieving goals, and making sure they do it correctly. This means that performers are able to accept anything less than 100%. This can lead them to be very successful in any endeavor they undertake. They know how to motivate others and help them overcome obstacles. They are great leaders which makes them exceptional in a variety of careers, including acting, business and sports.

The performer should simply allow life to happen, feel it, and let it take its course. To be able to draw their own conclusions, they must accept the challenges and celebrate all that life has to offer.

Type 4 The Romantic

The romantic type is all creative and uses art as a medium to express their thoughts, feelings, opinions and ideas. Different people use different methods to channel what's inside. Some people like the perfectionist prefer to keep it in themselves and focus on other aspects. The performer channels it into his work and to the high levels he achieves.

Romantic people have their own ways to express their feelings, thoughts and emotions. They do this through poetry, music and dance. Sentimental, elaborate and passionate about expressing one's thoughts. They feel passionate when they are able to switch between what others feel and what they feel. The romantics are emotional individuals that can comprehend emotions better than other personalities. This allows them reach people who may not have the same ability or to understand their emotions through art.

Because of their emotional nature, they need time to process and accept the situation before they can embrace the world. Because they are so emotionally charged, they need to be taken care of.

The romantic may have a dynamic mood. It could be either excited at times or drained depending on the task at hand. They live life with an open heart and are open to new experiences.

Romantics should balance all emotions. They need to understand that they are all there for a reason. You will get different reactions from them. They will learn different things which will help you have better conversations and problem solving skills.

Type 5 : The Observer

The Observer is the fifth personality that we will examine. These people are introverts. They are keen to see what is going on around them. They question everything they see and try to make sense of everything. The observer is more likely to focus on his own thoughts as he creates his ideas. The observer sees family and friends as being important but their own interests are more important. Due to their introverted sociological environments, they rarely engage in small talk. This is because they dislike sharing personal information and tend not to share it. They are drawn to the possibility of finding solutions and conclusions from the things they have seen and the analyses they have performed in their lives.

The observer hates small talk. They are more comfortable talking about and discussing topics that they are expert at. This is because they fear being unable to know the truth. Even though they're experts, they don't enjoy sharing all the information they have about a particular topic. It's possible they might be giving away too much 'valuable' information.

The Observers should be open to new ideas and accept more people. This will make them feel less lonely, and it will also help them expand their knowledge to include more topics that may interest them. Observers are extremely smart and highly valuable.

Type 6 The Loyal Skeptic

This group is distinguished by their ability both to judge people and situations and their ability solve problems before they happen. This group will always be looking out for people and situations which could bring harm to their loved one or family. They believe people have different attitudes and intentions. It is up to them, therefore, to understand and quickly find solutions. They aren't easy to trust but once they do, they trust extremely strongly. This makes them a great friend and a close friend.

Loyal skeptics are fast to think of solutions and remain ahead of the competition. This allows them more control over their lives and makes it easier for them make decisions. They either find a solution or stop it from happening. They act courageously and selflessly to ensure the safety of those they love.

They are strategic because they are highly attentive to people, situations and people. Every detail is essential in coming up to preventive or control measures. They put up walls that no one else should surpass in order to protect their emotional wellbeing. They are brave and often ask serious questions. This leads to them adopting aggressive or pushy behaviors.

Loyal Skeptics should embrace more emotions and opinions in their lives and be more open-minded to others. This will help them become better people and allow them to find a purpose that transcends their career. Overall, Type 6 is loyal, making them a wonderful friend and person to be around. They are smart and want to protect the people in their lives that they believe are worthy.

Type 7 - The Epicure

The seventh personality, the epicure is the dynamic crew. These people are open-minded and value freedom. These people are passionate about the experience and driven by exploration. Type 7's are driven to see new places, learn new skills, explore other continents, and live in every moment. They are never truly static.

This group is constantly striving to realize, achieve and explore. They have so much to offer and are great people to chat to and get to know. These are the reasons they should be valued. They are generally very likable people.

This group, however, is unfocused and undecided. Instead of focusing on one thing, they move around and find meaning. They only care about what they do best and won't let anyone's opinion affect them. They place a lot of emphasis on what they enjoy and work as hard as they can. They have a tendency to ignore their difficulties and concentrate on what's right. Epicure members should recognize that different people may have different opinions. The Epicure group should accept this fact as a fact, and then understand it completely. This will help them become better individuals and develop better skills.

Type 7s are inclined to think that "Everything happens to a reason" which is a powerful way to see the world.

Chapter 5: Testing The Personality Of The Enneagram

To determine the personality types discussed so far, it is important to answer several questions. These questions are intended to help you assess the personality and make an accurate assessment. There are many online personality tests you can choose from, both paid or free. They are all closely related. In order to avoid paying for a test you might take two or three free assessments. This chapter will concentrate on what the Enneagram testing looks for as well as the way it produces the results. It will also end with several examples questions. You won't find one of these tests in this book because they are so intense and require a lot more scoring. For the best reading experience, you can look online for it before you begin.

Enneagram Tests

This test can be used in conjunction with the Big Five personality and Myers-Briggs personality checks. It gives an additional aspect to an individual's ability to identify their true self. This test looks at the personality type of the person and considers how it interacts.

An individual's self-reporting is all that's used to create the Enneagram. Some people may be skeptical that it accurately describes a person's personality type. After all, look at several different personality disorders--narcissists believe that they are the most perfect, worthy of admiration people there could be, while those with BPD may believe that they are inherently flawed beyond repair, and that is why they believe they are constantly abandoned. This can lead to inaccurate perceptions of our personalities. It is possible that people report their ideal personality type, rather than the real person they are.

It is nevertheless an important tool. It is common to be given multiple traits in contrasting pair and then asked to rate which part of that spectrum you feel you belong. When you do this you are rating yourself on the trait and then it is compared to the traits of Enneagram type.

It is important to accurately answer an Enneagram exam. In order to give an accurate answer, it is important that you are honest with you self as you answer the questions. If you're unsure where to put yourself on a scale and how to answer a query, be honest with you self.

It Works

These tests will likely ask you more than 100 questions and score you accordingly. They usually take between 10 and 20 mins depending on your speed with reading and answering. Once you have finished answering all the questions, your score will be calculated to determine how closely they relate to your personality type. Your dominant type is the type with which you are closest.

Some people may find an answer that is unexpected or not what they expected. Even though you may have believed that you were an Observer or a Perfectionist, it turns out that this was not the case. Remember that you took the test to find out what your results would be. You need to be open-minded and understand that although we may believe we know ourselves best, it is still possible that you have misinterpreted our beliefs.

Your results are likely to be accurate if the test was honest. Instead of getting annoyed or upset about the results, you should think about the benefits that you have received by simply learning the truth. You will soon be able to identify your greatest weaknesses because you now know the truth. You will be able see your strengths. By learning your strengths and weaknesses, you can improve your relationships.

Criticisms on the Enneagram

As already stated, it can be hard to get reliable evidence and results when tests are subjective. A subjective test can be seen as imperfection by one person, while another person may perceive it as something quite different. Despite being a good at handling people, you may feel shy. This could cause some discrepancies. For example, someone might identify themselves as a Type 1 individual while another person with the same personality characteristics and a different point of view may achieve a completely different result.

Other people

Another criticism of Enneagram involves the belief that it is completely based on pseudoscience. This is because they believe that only a few questions could reduce someone to a personality that has the exact same tendencies. But, this tool isn't scientific. It is not intended to be used to diagnose individuals, but instead is a tool that can help you reflect on your own self and gain insight into your true self. It should not serve as a therapeutic tool. Instead, because it can provide valuable information for those who might not know who they really are, it should not be used. Despite it not being peer-reviewed, it is valid and necessary because of the insight that people gain.

Finally, personality types could be just as vague and ambiguous as horoscopes. They are believed to fall under the Barnum

Effect. In this case, something is just vaguely relatable enough to allow people to see meaning where none is. This is also the method used by scammers to convince people to believe they can forecast their fortunes. They use vague statements that allow it to hold true for a variety of situations. People take that to mean something.

This is not a diagnostic method. It is meant to help you gain personal insight, and not be used in any kind of psychological process. It is a valuable resource if it is used as a personal tool to self-discovery.

Question Examples

At this point, we'll go over some sample questions from an Enneagram test. These questions are yours to answer as you go. Take the time to answer them all.

You can indicate your opinion on the accuracy or inaccuracy of the following statement by using a scale between 1-5. Let 1 not be accurate, 3 be neutral, 5 be accurate.

I do my best in trying to help.

I must achieve what I set forth to do and not fail.

I want other people like me
I feel a variety emotions
I am a deep and philosophical thinker
I feel unat ease and out of place.
No matter what happens I am always prepared
I am able to find something positive no matter how terrible the situation.
I domineer over decision-making
I often get lost in daydreams
Pick which statement you think is more accurate.
More value is placed on:
Things getting done when promised
It's okay to have fun even when you don't finish your work
As:
Exciting, positive
Concerning the positive and the negative
I make every effort to ensure that
Everyone is on task
Everyone has had all their needs met
I normally:

Avoid dwelling on the past, especially when it has been difficult
Moving on is the best thing you can do.
I want my name to be known as:
I am successful, accomplished and have met my goals
Unique and memorable
I want to:
Make a statement in the crowd
Incorporate yourself into the crowd
It is the following that I value most:
My relationships
My work and success
When angry, I:
Struggle for anger to be expressed to others
You don't have to be angry with me
I'm more interested in:
My feelings over those of other people
Over my own feelings, I prefer the opinions of other people
People are awestruck by my:
Intelligence and knowledge
My toughness or persistence
To the following statements, answer true or False:

I am never or rarely depressed.

I am too strict

Even though I may not be able to know them well or in depth, I tend to trust people.

I find it very rewarding to take care of others. I really excel at this.

I want to be successful and recognized at all costs.

For me to truly enjoy a sport or play a game, I need it to win

In intimate interpersonal and romantic relationships, I give more than i take.

It is difficult for my to stay focused and complete my work on time, especially when there is something I would prefer to do.

My office and my home are always neat and tidy. I value order and organization.

I am romantic by heart and will show that in relationships

There will be many questions in the online tests. Some may have several dozen questions. For each of the nine traits that you test for, there will be several dozen questions. This is to give you an idea of how close you can relate to each Enneagram type.

Chapter 6: Enneagram Self-Discovery

The Enneagram personality classification system is very dynamic. It's also very insightful. People naturally gravitate towards one type of dominant personality. Knowing yourself can help you see the impact of your character traits on your life. Knowing this will help you make the right changes to realize your goals. Once you are able to recognize the patterns you've been following, it will be easier to understand each of these personality types. You need to get to know each type of personality. Awareness is the first step to self-discovery. Once you're aware of how you behave, you can begin to make improvements. Let us now learn more about each type of personality.

Type 1 The Perfectionist

Type One is also known by the names of the Perfectionist or the Reformer. True to form, they are more difficult on themselves than any other personality type. They tend to be extremely critical of themselves and never take a moment to rest. They are sometimes wise and able to discern the truth. They can be stubborn and picky. Typ Ones may strive for perfection, which is sometimes impossible. They not only set high standards but also have high expectations for others. They are responsible and do their best to make others happy.

Aside from that, they have impossibly high moral standards. They are an excellent example for what integrity and ethics should look. It is clear that the world can use more Ones.

They might strive for perfection but this doesn't make them invincible. They fear being wrong. Ones love to be right, and they are not afraid to make mistakes. They can be rational, idealistic, principled, and productive when at their best. They are reform-minded. They constantly think of new ways to improve their lives. They possess the mind of a perfectionist. They are organized and very emotional. At their worst, they can be inflexible, judgmental of other people and themselves as well as hypocritical and self-righteous. No matter what others think, one believes that they can be objective and reasonable.

Ones have three key motivators: living upto their high standards, being efficient, and excelling in all they do. They seek to be fair in all of their dealings and want to make the world more beautiful.

This personality type doesn't sound too appealing to be true. It is possible that the attributes that they find most beneficial are also the ones that can hinder their personal growth. Type One personalities can include famous celebrities such as Al Gore (Gandhi), Gandhi, Hillary Clintons, Jerry Brown, Margaret Thatchers, Joan Baez and Katharine Hepburn.

All you Ones out on the planet, this is my message: You are fine if you do what is right. You can set high standards for yourself and others. But, this can cause you a lot of problems. Actually, half of your problems could be solved if you let yourself have some fun. Give yourself a break. Everyone deserves it.

Type 2 The Helper

Type 2, also called the Helpers (or the Type 2), is good at giving and not so great at receiving. They are generous and will always help others. They love helping others because it gives them the feeling of being needed. They want to be needed. Because of their helpful and generous nature, all Twos are attracted like honey to honey. They are willing to help others and do so without expectation. They make great counselors. They are open-minded and can be a great counselor. They see the good in people.

All Twos share three core beliefs. They believe that everyone should consider the needs of others more than their own. They should always offer if they would like to be rewarded. The third belief is that they must strive hard to win the affection of others. These are the beliefs that all three of the Twos strongly believe. These are the opinions that they have held since childhood. If you have these three beliefs, you're probably a Two. Twos feel it is selfish to take care of their own needs.

That's kind of sad. It isn't all selfless. They have needs and expectations. However, they are afraid of acknowledging their needs. Melanie Hamilton in Gone with the Wind is a perfect example of a Type Two personality.

Their primary fear is feeling unloved or unwanted. They cannot bear the thought of not being loved. Twos feel loved and supported, so they are not happy to be alone. They long to feel loved. Twos are at their best when they are caring, nurturing, and loving. Twos can be a bit possessive and manipulative when they are at their worst. They can be very domineering and can cause problems. They may not be aware they are manipulative. They believe they love people and are compassionate.

Twos desire unconditional love and want to share it. Their motivation to succeed is fueled by the desire to be loved and respected. Numerous famous personalities such as Eleanor Roosevelt. Barbara Bush. Bishop Desmond Tutu. Albert Schweitzer. Leo Buscaglia Jr. Ann Landers. Sammy Davis. Nancy Reagan. John Denver. Dolly

Parton. Florence Nightingale. Luciano Pavarotti.

To all the Twos out in the world, my message is that you can let others love your. To feel loved, it doesn't necessarily mean that you must do something. It's OK to receive, even when you aren't giving. Learn to be a gracious giver. Understanding the difference in needing and loving is crucial. Love and need are two different things. Understanding the difference will help you feel more at ease. Expectations are fine. Your expectations should be acknowledged. It is impossible to read minds and everyone will be different. At times, you might have to communicate your expectations with people. However, it doesn't make someone shallow or selfish. You need to stop thinking like this.

Type 3 The Achiever

Type Three comprises all the performers and go getters. They want to grow and develop others. Type Threes take great pleasure in achieving their goals, which is a contrast to other personality types. They are often successful, and they can motivate themselves to accomplish their goals. Threes are defined by their family culture, their values and their personal definitions. For some, a large family can indicate success. While for others, a great education might mean success. Threes want their community and family to consider them a success, regardless what definition they have of success. Threes are almost always focused on achieving their goals in life. They can be very persuasive and will do anything to get the attention and praise that they need. Threes invest a lot in activities that provide value to their families and peers during their childhood. They are influenced by others' definitions of success to determine their self-worth. They will feel completely empty if they are not successful. Do you remember Don Dapper in Mad Men? He is an example of a type-three personality.

The greatest fear of all Threes is feeling worthless. They don't want to see their lives without the success which they love. Their primary goal is to feel worthwhile and valuable. They are authentic, confident, motivated, focused, and self-assured. They can be very pretentious, calculating, deceptive, and even pretentious at their worst. They seek success, even if it means losing the end. They want others to think they are great. It is wrong to think that others will make them successful.

Threes are motivated by the goals they set. They want fame and visibility. Their success is everything. Famous personalities such as Oprah Winfrey. Bill Clinton. Paul McCartney. Tom Cruise. Barbra Streisand. Michael Jordan. Shirley MacLaine. Denzel Washington. Tiger Woods. John Edwards.

To all Threes: You shouldn't allow others to determine your worth. Don't allow anyone to tell you otherwise. Your strengths are what make you unique. You should do the things that make you happy. They are not cool if others think so. If you let others make the decisions about your happiness, you won't find true happiness. You have the right to choose your path and you can believe in yourself. Don't try to live life according to what others expect. It's important to take the time to reflect on what you value and what you are looking for. Without your success, what are you worth?

Eleven tips on how to behave with the Nine Enneagram

These are just a few things that you can do if you want to live a happier, more fulfilling life. Here are ten ways to make your life happier.

1.Everything in your life won't go as planned. There will be setbacks. You will experience some setbacks. You might screw things up. Being too focused on things and making your happiness dependent upon them will only make you miserable. Whatever happens, you have to learn how to be content. People will often put others in their path. This is often done without realizing. This is why you should not worry about a certain outcome.

2.Unpredictable events will happen. Only you can control what happens to you. It is impossible to control the circumstances in which you live. Do not worry about how you can achieve a particular result. Instead, be focused on the ways you can make the best of what you're given. If you put too much effort into achieving a desired result, it will only lead to frustration. If you don't have the will to succeed, you won't get the results that are yours. It will slow down your growth. Do not try and fit in where you do not belong. It's time to find a shoe that fits you. Find something you're comfortable with.

3. No two people can be alike. Why should we have one standard of success? We end up becoming stuck in the race the society has set for us to attain the "rules" of success. There will always a better person than you at some thing. There is never enough time to do it all. Instead, concentrate on the things you do.

4. You have simultaneously rejected other things when you select one thing. It is part of everyday life, and it is completely acceptable to do so. It is quite liberating to choose what it is that you like. You are responsible for defining what happiness,

success and wealth mean to your life. You cannot allow society to dictate what you require or want. If that happens, you'll always be lacking something. Stop comparing your self to others and don't compete with other people. It is the only way that you will succeed in your daily life. Grab yourself out from the endless rat race or the rut you are stuck.

5. How often have you said "just one" to yourself? Most people have convinced themselves that they can break their own rules. We find reasons to justify the small decisions we make. These aren't big decisions at first. These decisions eventually become a part and parcel of the bigger picture. Human beings are capable of self-sabotage. People often behave against their goals or contrary to their ideals. It should not be difficult to find a gap between what is happening and what you should. The smaller your gap between what you do and what you should be doing, the more happy you will feel in life. Giving 100 percent commitment will be

more comfortable than giving only 98 percent.

6. When you have fully committed yourself to something, this is a sign that it has been done. You will always be a victim to the outside circumstances of life unless you are 100% committed. If you depend on your willpower, you are more likely to fall apart. You might feel that you do more than you do. However, once you have made your commitment to 100 percent, it is not enough to believe that you are doing better than you actually are. It doesn't matter what circumstances you face, your decision is made. It's important to be proactive instead of reactive.

7. Abundance and lack can exist simultaneously in one's life. It is our choice to decide which of these items we want. Happiness is simply a decision to place your attention on the positive aspects of your life rather than on things that are lacking. It could be as simple and as simple as being grateful for what you have. Research suggests that gratitude can lead to specific physical, psychological, as well

as social benefits. These include a stronger immune, reduced body aches, pains, better circulation, and better sleep. These psychological benefits include increased happiness and optimism. You'll feel more alert, happier, and more positive.

8. Your social benefits will include feeling more caring, generous, compassionate and forgiving. People are generally not grateful for all of these benefits. People tend to put too much emphasis on what isn't there. The grass always looks greener on the opposite side. If you achieve something, there will always be another. There is an endless list of desires. Life has become an endless race for the best. If all you want in your life is more, how can you ever be happy? Enjoy what you have.

9.Be mindful of the language you speak. People who are grateful tend to use more words such as gifts, abundance and blessings. When you start to include these words in your daily vocabulary, it will be easy to see how many things you need to be thankful for. It will allow to you to recognize and appreciate all that you have.

Smile often, and be grateful for the kindness of others. This could be as simple and as straightforward as acknowledging that someone opened the door for you.

10. It's a smart strategy to use the opportunities we have to be the best version of ourselves. There are so many things in life that are wonderful and great. However, that does not mean you need to do them all. Every day is a chance to seize once-in-a lifetime opportunities.

11.People tend to grab every opportunity that comes along, even when it's not in line with their vision of life. It is the reason people move in different directions. They are not able to think straight and can't see the way. People who are happy will turn down any opportunity they see, no matter how extraordinary, as long their inner peace is maintained. They won't be willing to sacrifice their freedoms for the sake security. They will not be distracted by distractions. There are very few things in life that are truly "best". You can only choose the best. Don't get distracted with "good activities" and lose out on the wonderful ones.

Happy people are those that live in today. They don't forget the moments that really matter. They are thankful for what they have. Happy people put emphasis on the most important aspects in their lives.

Chapter 7: How can I figure out which type of personality I am?

The Enneagram (or Enneagram) is a wonderful character writing tool used by teachers and others. The Enneagram reveals nine types of personality and three bands (or concentrates) of comprehensions. These include heart disease, gut and gut. Each group of three will have 3 personality types.

The middle set includes 3 types of untruths 3, 2, and 4. Type two is that of the Giver. Type 3 is that of the Performer. And type 4 is that the Romantic (also called "Sad Romantic"). All of these types feel at ease with their sense focal point or the centre.

All three types possess a passion for thermometers. They travel the globe and analyze every single person they catch. They can almost see inside the room when they come to a certain area. They feel concerned about how they are feeling.

How are they responding? What are they truly happy about?

Types 3, 2 and 4 – it's all about Picture

Types 3, 2 and 4 will represent the core tern and are therefore located. They are totally comfortable and feel linked to the world through their atmosphere.

They aren't content with your responses and ardent material. They are constantly changing their minds because they're worried about your response to them. They are constantly changing themselves to see the passionate responses. Each of these three types seem different when they succeed.

Types 2, 3, and 4 believe that they are worthy of admiration or feeling valued. Their inner feeling of self is, in a huge way, dependent on what's being reflected back. This is how they discover their identity. This is usually where their thoughts are drawn to: towards others' reaction to them. They are based upon what they do and say, as well as the way that they expect and conduct themselves. It's about appearances.

The "photograph thing", as it is known, continues inexorably. It shows in their energy, in how they walk, and in the way that precede. It can be seen in the terminology they use.

Sort 4 is associated with what someone may say or do that will make them feel unwell. They are able to react in a huge way to this.

Typ 2's pay attention to the feelings of the other person and what's transpiring. They want to ask "How can I help you?" It's fully tuned; it is called the Picture Point. Because they create their image by how others react.

You will find bitterness underneath the exteriors of 2's-3's and 4's. As they start their job, most will see the hidden signs of their identity, and they will be reimbursed hard by yet another person.

Their Contemplations are based on the idea that there is something deeper than me. You might discover that the internal imperfections are hidden. They could enter, but not quite as close. They might be able to find the answer."

Types 5, 6, and 7, the Emotional Triad

Types 5, 6 & 7 are the head-based types. They include underlining of fear, anxiety, and fear.

They are at home in the worlds they have created. Their mental movement helps them to control their mind and be well.

Their Concerns say: "Up in mind. I will try to get it. I will carefully consider everything. I can make a version about how this planet functions. After pushing my version onto Earth, I start taking that version more gradually.

The Mental types can be strategic, often being adroit. They have a marginal understanding of the world and the social contexts. They are currently working on the eyes. They're seeing and visiting to examine the reactions to speeches.

All mind types have a basic earth matter. There's an institution for those 5 who get too close. In this way, queries are generated and they can escape the world for a piece of their work.

Sort 6 is moving outward and inward. Their question is still open to the public.

They feel that they cannot trust the market. However, there is an inner sense to this, and they feel, "I cannot trust market." Thus, there's a lot polarity within sixes.

The 7 is a higher volume of an externalized faith. Their focus of attention is outside on Earth. This can cause them to lose their position but not feel good about it. These feelings, along with the nerves, may manifest on Earth as a result of their fear or anxiety. They will be able to do so indoors gradually.

Types 8, 9 & 1 - Human Body/Gut

Types 8, 9 or 9 will be human body (or intestinal)-based types. They feel things all over the body. They make energetic hits. They can be seen walking to space. However, it's not about the feeling of believing.

Types indicate that the body has hidden displeasure, or disdain. This often manifests as ruling. Type 9's outrage can be subdued and they will not allow it to go outside. Even more, they become subdued in their demands.

On the off chance that you have to speak with a "young 9," they will likely reply, "Outrage. What exactly are you talking about?" I am the calmest, most articulate and giddy person I know. I don't know what it means to be outraged.

It may be so, however, that their outrage grows and becomes apparent as they move deeper into themselves. They'll discover an extraordinary level of mindfulness as well as articulation. They will have no other example to guide them in understanding their needs and what they want.

Sort 8 will often externalize outrage. Their energy is much higher, and it ends. It can be overwhelming and it can lead to outrage throughout the world. They have no sense of limitations and are often unable to accept them. They enjoy expressing their discontent outside and are open to the possibility of others doing the same.

Sort 1 turns bitterness into something internal. They will describe an internal pundit, which is making a determination about the gender of the person they are riding. It is usually saying, "You have got to do it along such lines." This is the reason you got lost. You're moronic. It is not right. Your senses aren't full. You're not stimulated enough. You aren't (anything) enough.

This is a hidden displeasure, but it can often be quite judgmental. There is an insubordinate part for them. Type 1 will tend to feel discontent in their bodies.

These are the "Focuses" of Intelligence: The centre (Types 3, 4, and 5 using a hidden trouble or disgrace), as well as the mind and body (types 6, 7 and 8 using basic dread, uneainess, and type 9 with fundamental bitterness/judgment).

Self-learning Can be very fun. The Enneagram is also a great tool to show you important parts of yourself. It may give you information about your trends, which will help you decide what options you'll choose. It may also provide information about your deepest life goals, your needs, and particularly your qualities. Your qualities can help you identify what you are looking for and allow you to clarify the objectives.

It will, however, not tell you everything you think it should. The report does not give much information about your abilities.

The Enneagram Could Provide the Similar Benefits Throughout Your Own Life and Work

* It promotes mindfulness, significant contemplation, and mindful awareness

* Lets You See the World from Other Points of View

* It lets one form positive and new practices

* It helps you understand and break down illustrations

* It motivates you to be more understanding and caring for others

Chapter 8: Type One Personality

Type One (reformer and perfectionist, achiever) - Type 1s are willing to work hard and sacrifice in order to reach their goals. They want to see things done correctly and they are a perfectionist.

Type Ones exhibit the following characteristics:

*They value the rules and regulations that have been laid down and they give priority to their compliance, on both an individual as well as group level. They feel guilty and hurt when they do not meet the high standards set for them and others. They are also committed to improving themselves, identifying and fixing their flaws and imperfections, and working towards them becoming better. If not careful measures are taken to rein in their excesses, the Type One personality could become an autoritarian.

*Type 1 personalities like to set the example and keep things on track. They want everything to go according to plan and bring order to the environment. They have a tendency for micromanaging their subordinates and paying attention to every little detail, especially when they're in a leadership position. They can be managed easily depending on who their leader or manager is. They will often find themselves in conflict with their superiors if they don't care much about procedures or rules.

*Type Ones are part of the physical and instinctual groups. They can see problems even when others cannot. They see past the surface and can spot issues that could lead to serious consequences. They are also keen to take preventative measures to address the problem before it escalates. They won't hesitate to accept responsibility and don't fear facing any challenge.

*Type Ones are good at relating and inter-acting with others. They excel in working together in groups to achieve common objectives. They are naturally leaders, and they are not afraid to take the lead. They can also be very independent when they need to and only show their social side to attain specific goals. They are more likely to keep their word and follow the agreements they make with others.

*Type Ones possess high self-esteem and moral values. They are looking for conformity and support from others in order to do the "right things" at all times. They want to follow the rules. If things aren't in line with these rules, they will trigger them. Type One personalities are those who hold high standards and have integrity. These people won't accept shortcuts to reach their goals, no matter how many chances are available.

*Type one is comfortable working in high pressure situations with strict deadlines. They thrive on being challenged to achieve desirable results that meet both individual and group goals. They are sometimes very judgmental of others, and even their own self. Self-criticism helps them achieve remarkable results that others may not be capable of achieving if given the same opportunities and resources.

*Type Ones make great time and planning managers. They are organised and have a clear idea about what they want done for the week, month and year ahead. They enjoy working with people who have a good sense of organization and can help them to make tangible progress on their assigned tasks. Their hallmark is punctuality. They don't like it when they miss a meeting or an occasion. Types like a boring life. They can be bored by monotonous tasks.

*Type Ones will be strict parents who set very clear standards and guidelines for their children. Type One parents often punish children who fail to follow their rules. They can be more strict if they were raised by Type One parents. Type Ones have a balanced approach to work and life. They invest time and resources in both and are committed to making their lives fulfilling.

Below is the list of Type Ones who have been admired throughout human history.

Abraham Lincoln - 16th President, United States. He led America during the Civil war (the worst moral and constitutional crisis in American History). As a Type one, he worked towards maintaining the Union, abolishing the slavery, strengthening central government and modernising economy. He advocated reforms (like the abolition and strengthening of the central government) that would normalize affairs in a country context and propel the country forward.

Nelson Mandela (South African political leader, peace activist. Revolutionary and philanthropist. He is revered as an icon for democracy and social justice. He was also awarded the Nobel Peace Prize. As a Type I, he brought down apartheid in South Africa and secured the rights to the black majority. He spent 27 year behind bars and was willing sacrifice his life to support institutional reforms.

George Bernard Shaw - an Irish playwright. A critic and political activist, Shaw became the foremost dramatist his generation. Shaw also had a significant influence on culture, politics and theatre in western Europe. He was awarded the Nobel Prize in Literature in 1925. He was a Type 1 and was well-known as a vocal critic on a wide variety of issues such as vaccination, eugenics or alphabet reform. He took sides in the First World War.

Martin Luther - Martin Luther is a German professor priest, composer, monk and priest who led the Protestant Reformation. It resulted a secessionist movement from the Roman Catholic Catholic Church, and gave birth to major Protestant denominations throughout the world. His Type One abilities were shown in leading the Protestant Reformation to overthrow the Roman Catholic Church. He rejected many of their teachings. Luther refused to denounce their writings. This led to Luther being excommunicated and condemned by Pope Benedict XVI.

Thomas Moore - Irish poet and singer. His music has been a lasting legacy in Europe, America and Europe. Thomas Moore was an advocate of ending slavery in all forms. He made this a consistent theme in his writings concerning the United States. His mocking criticisms often resulted in rebuttals. Moore wanted a world where all were free and equal.

Charles Dickens was a Victorian great novelist. This English writer, social critic, enjoyed huge popularity throughout his life. By the close of the 20thcentury both scholars and critics had identified him as an English literary genius. Type Ones share a similar obsession with perfection. He published his novels every other week and used his audience's reactions to improve his plot and character building in subsequent publications. In his writings, he often expressed his views on the need to reform socio-economical or labour conditions because of his warehouse work.

Oliver Cromwell (an English military and politics leader) was the Lord Protector of England Scotland Ireland. He then became both the acting head of country and head of government of the newly established republic. After a religious conversion, Cromwell became an independent Puritan. This allowed him to have a more tolerant view of the various Protestant sects he encountered.

Margaret Thatcher — A British stateswoman who served as the longest-serving British prime Minister and was also the first woman in that position. Due to her uncompromising political and leadership style, she was sometimes called "The Iron Lady." She was an active politician from her teens and was often regarded as a potential prime minister. These are the Type One characteristics she displayed.

Type Ones often play the roles of -

The Umpire Type One likes to enforce the rules within any group where given the opportunity. They will call any player who errs. They prefer to be objective or neutral in deciding matters when they are called to do so.

The Teacher - Type Ones wants to show everyone how things should go. In this context, "everyone" means everyone. This can include acquaintances as well as strangers, family members, friends, superiors, and subordinates. Some people might see them as wanting a professor-like approach when there is a lot to discuss.

Paragon Type Ones enjoy being a role model. They want to be admired by their group as an example of excellence.

Critic — Type Ones speak out when things aren't right or seem wrong. They want to see the return of the status-quo and the ideal way to do things. When it comes down to faults or weaknesses in how things are done, these people can be vocal. They may not be able to accept the faults or weaknesses of others.

The Idealist is - They seem like they have a great idea of how things should go. They expect others to live up to their standards. They won't be afraid to pursue high and noble goals no matter what.

The Puritan- They favor simplicity and a modest life style and so flamboyance is not something they stand for. They are generally strict about religious issues and will uphold very high moral standards.

Cleric - Type ones would make every effort to spread the gospel of moral and religious concerns to others. You could see them displaying a holier than thou attitude that can put people off and leave a bad impression.

Fundamentalists - From a religious standpoint, they are likely function as fundamentalists. This means that they adhere to the core doctrines and tenets in their faith. They will defend the faith they believe in to the end, provided they feel that they are doing the right and moral thing.

The Rulemaker - These people are exceptional at writing regulations and rules for people to use. They have a clear vision of how things should be and are able incorporate these ideas in the formulation and application of applicable laws.

The Advocate – Type Ones will easily fit in to the position of an advocate. They push for things done right. Their personality type fits the role of a legislator.

Type Ones are driven to perfection and always strive to improve their surroundings and themselves. One can describe the positive side of a Type One with words such as productive, honest, ethical, diligent, hard-working, orderly, reliable and consistent. There are many adjectives that can describe the negative side of a Type 1: judgmental, obstinate, rigid, rigid and anxious.

One would be most at home in the following fields: law enforcement, medicine, engineering, law enforcement and banking.

Type One personalities, who are perfectionists or reformers in Enneagram's Enneagram model, want everything to be perfect. They want to have a home for everything and be able see everything.

In this chapter, the following are examined:

* Characteristic traits of Type One personalities

*Famous Type One personalities in history

*Typical roles that a Type 1 personality could take on

Chapter 9: Enneagram You and Us

Let us add another layer of complexity to our understanding of relationships.

Our chances of becoming more focused, thoughtful, and thoughtful are higher when we're happy.

Pay attention to our cognitive and behavioral selves. We have the right to choose how we want to behave.

Take action. The Enneagram offers us a way of identifying strengths and eliminating weaknesses.

It is possible to conceal your weaknesses. You can learn so much from others.

It is vital to remember that improving relationships does not depend on how old they are.

All parties involved should be open to discussing their feelings, whether they're romantic, professional, or friend.

You can be compassionate about the needs of others and listen to them. Our experiences are ours to share.

We must be able to understand and sympathize with the people around us. Researchers all around the globe

We tried to find common ground between gender roles, demographics, and values.

For those who are looking for the "aha!" moment that will reveal why some relationships work,

fail. These efforts can be inconsistent and result in mixed results.

This is just a small sample of the many types you could use.

Learn from the Enneagram. You will find more specific information.

You can improve your relationships by using the centuries-old concept called the Enneagram in all areas.

The Enneagram has a wonderful asset: it doesn't tell you which person should be.

drawn to one another by numbers. It instead allows for the possibility of different

Different types can be attracted to each other in a healthy stage.

collection of positive qualities. Because an individual isn't held captive anymore, by their innate or reactive impulses but strengthened through awareness and knowledge

These are more acceptable behaviours and responses.

We can set and visualize our goals, and we can achieve them. Modern.

Mnemonics make setting goals easier and more tangible

*S - Specific

* M – Measurable

* A - Attainable

* R = Realistic

* T – Timely

Make use of the Enneagram results you have collected about yourself

It's universal to apply it to the steps for setting your goals. It is a great tool to help you reach your goals.

You can enhance your self-esteem, build relationships, and help others succeed in school and at work.

Research supporting the Enneagram's spiritual and psychological aspects has led to a lot more research.

These applications are intimate. A new trend supports this.

The process can be used by business to solve problems and increase business profits for both.

Managers and employees.

Chapter 10: The Enneagram Personality type 5 - The Observer

This personality type also goes by the name Investigator. This personality type is often called the Investigator. This person likes to sit and watch, but then they want to get involved in new situations, new activities, or new people. They do this to avoid being considered incompetent, unprepared, and emotionally depleted by disengagement.

What makes The Observer a Great Personality?

The Observer can be alert and insightful. This personality type seeks to understand how things work. This person desires to know more about their environment. This knowledge will help them protect themselves from the dangers in their environment. This personality is constantly searching and asking questions. This person does more than accept other people's opinions. Instead, they conduct their own investigations. They are mentally solid and have a high level of intelligence. Many of them are scientifically oriented so they express themselves in the areas that appeal to them.

The Observer often becomes an expert in a chosen field. Observers are usually relentless in their pursuit for knowledge. This allows them the ability to master multiple subject areas and interests.

The Observer is independent, creative, and innovative. This personality type does away with external validation. Therefore, they are very independent in how they think and live their lives. These people are visionaries due to their vast understanding of the world, its structure and its inhabitants.

The Observer does not have the ability to manipulate. Type 5s don't have an agenda and often just want to get along with someone.

The Deadly Sins of the Observer

The Observer fears becoming incompetent and useless. This person is the epiphany that thinking before doing. Behind their ability lies a deep sense of insecurity, which stems from being perceived as helpless and unworthy by others.

The Observer is able to isolate himself. This person is more comfortable in the realms or thought than they are in real life. They don't feel confident in their ability and abilities to deal with reality. They will withdraw to the safety zone of their minds to prepare mentally to deal with people, situations, events, and other people. Type 5s also tend to be reluctant to seek help from others, even when they know that these people would be happy to assist them. These types of people want to be self-sufficient.

The Observer tends to be preoccupied by their imagination and thoughts. Although they are highly intelligent, Observers can have difficulty taking the information they gather and putting it into action. Because they concentrate so much of their energy mental, Observers often neglect their bodies, minds, and spirits. Their insatiable search for more information sometimes leads them to neglect their bodies, hearts, and spirits, and thus miss out a lot of life's experiences.

The Observer is emotionally distant. Observers are comfortable in the realms thought and feel less connected when it comes to emotions. They can have difficulty with relationships and avoid deep connections. They do this because they are sensitive and feel incapable of handling the demands of a romantic relationship. This can lead towards loneliness. As a result, they tend to be intellectually arrogant or indifferent. While this helps them to cope, it often leads to emotional distance and can be hard to heal. Type 5s often have long-lasting relationships if they can make deep, meaningful connections with other people. Type 5s can feel deeply even though they struggle with emotional expression. A deep need to protect their privacy and fear of intrusion are two of the reasons that many people do not realize the extent of what is happening beneath the surface. Type 5s prefer to live a simple life so that they can communicate with others as little as possible.

The Observer lacks security. The Observer's drive to find knowledge stems from the fact that they feel ill-equipped and unable to work in the real world. They feel inferior in their ability to do things the way other people do. Instead of facing fear, they retreat into the safety of their minds. They pretend to be able to think for themselves and come out of it better prepared.

How observer relationships relate to other personality types

Observers in comparison to. Type 1

See Chapter 2, How Reformers are Related to Other Personality Styles: Reformers and Others. Type 5s.

Observers in comparison to. Type 2

Please refer to Chapter 3, How Helpers are Related to Other Personality Types. Helpers vs. Type 5s.

Observers in comparison to. Type 3

Please see Chapter 4. How Performers are Related to Other Personality Styles: Performers. Type 5s.

Types 4 vs. types 2 Observers

Please see Chapter 5 - How Artists Are Related to Other Personality Styles: Artists. Type 5s.

Types 6 vs. the Observers

These personality types, both mental, value accuracy and objectivity. They also value the ability to analyse situations without being biased. The Observer is a more emotional type. Type 6s, on the other hand, are more sympathetic and look to authority in the Observer. Loyalist's devotion and loyalty can break the Observer's tendency of isolation. Problems can arise from the fact that both personality types think differently. This can result in them ending up on opposite ends, which can cause a breakdown of trust and communication.

Types 7s vs. Observers

Both of these personalities are thought-provoking and enjoy bringing new ideas to the relationship. The Observer brings perspective, objectivity and clarity of observation to the relationship. Type 7, on the other hand, can bring the excitement for life, spontaneity, and insight that the Observer needs. Type 5s are prone to emotional retreat when stressed. Type 7s go into hyperdrive and can become more emotionally. These different coping mechanisms for dealing with emotional stimuli may cause rifts in relationships.

Types 8s and Observers

This combination of personality types makes a great pair because it complements each other and helps to balance out each other. Type 8s have to be more aware of what their actions are having on others and to think about the implications of those actions. Type 5s need a greater awareness of their bodies, and how they relate to their environment. Both types complement each other in a healthy relationship. Both personality types can be sensitive and easily rejected. This can cause problems in the relationship. Both personality types are susceptible to being cynical. This can lead to communication breakdowns.

Types 9s and Observers

The relationship between these personality types can work well because they each have their own unique personalities and are open to each other's emotional and personal space. One is neither intrusive and the other hovers. Respect for each others' boundaries, individuality, independence, and non-intrusiveness is the hallmark of such a relationship. It is possible for the two personalities to be too close, which can lead both to become distant.

How the Observer can improve his or her life

This personality type needs more awareness of their emotions and spirituality. They should realize that connecting with people, engaging emotionally in experiences, and getting outside their heads can make life more pleasant.

Yoga is a great method to connect with your emotions. Child's pose is a great position to achieve this. For this pose, you will need to sit down on your knees, kneel on your heels, and let your big feet touch the ground. Exhale as you place your torso between your knees and allow your tailbone a lengthen. Keep your thumbs in front of your thumbs, and lay your hands on a flat surface. Keep this position for at most 30 seconds. Allow your mind to clear out. You can breathe in and exhale deeply, and each breath will flow through your entire body.

You can try chakra meditations for this personality type to be more grounded in your present moment and feel more connected with your emotions. Acupressure may also prove to be beneficial. An acupressure specialist can stimulate the points SP-6 & ST36. To increase emotion and sense of feeling, TB-5 can easily be stimulated. It can be found just below the wristcrease on the upper arm. KI-6 lowers the effects fear has on the body. It is located in the inner part of the foot, below the ankle bone.

There are other ways the Observer could improve people's lives, such as:

* Being aware of when your mental functioning is impaired can allow you to live in the present.

* Staying connected with the present

* Use exercise to channel nervousness energy.

* Never use drugs or alcohol to relax.

* Take more decisive actions to improve self-confidence.

* Learning to handle conflict, not by withdrawing emotionally, but by finding healthy ways to solve it.

* Take the time to get more social and connect with others.

* Learning to trust other people.

Chapter 11: Type Six, The Loyalist

Sixes have a strong commitment to their fellow sixes and are committed to safety and security. Healthy Sixes may be more engaged and responsible. Lower functioning Sixes tend to be more suspicious and anxious.

Sixes are reliable and trustworthy, hardworking, responsible, and trustworthy. They are able anticipate problems and quickly respond to them to solve them. Sometimes, they can be too cautious, leading to indecisiveness.

Sixes are too consumed with their thoughts and the "what-ifs" to have confidence that their decisions will be made. They start to worry about what might occur. Most times, they imagine worse scenarios than what is actually likely to occur.

Sixes become anxious when problems become too overwhelming. They resort to defensiveness and evasion to deal with their anxiety.

Sixes suffer from self-doubt as well as suspicion. They need guidance and support to feel secure in their choices.

Sixes are faithful to a fault. Sixes will not let go of a relationship for any reason, good or bad. Sometimes they even hold on to it for too long. They are willing to stay for the long term, even if things get difficult and even if their loved ones have to suffer. They will stand up for their beliefs, their family, or their community more than any personal gain.

While most Sixes follow the herd and are loyal to others' beliefs and ideas. Some Sixes may venture out to be revolutionary or rebellious.

Sixes may be defined by the contradictory way they behave.

Sixes can be depending on their situation:

Strong and weak

Trusting and distrusting

Fearless and courageous

Both provokers and protectors

Sweet and sour

Bully and weak

Aggressive or passive

Offensive, defensive and mixed

Social and solo

Believers and doubters

Tender and kind

Both cooperative and obstructionist

Generous and petty

Sixes must be able to confront their fears, and learn to accept them before they can become calm and confident in any situation.

Sixes armed with a Five-Wing or Seven-Wing are known collectively as "The Defender," while those with a Sixes-Wing can be called "The Buddy".

Stress Point

Type Sixes might exhibit unhealthy or unhealthy levels of growth when they're stressed.

These unhealthy traits include:

Image-Conscious

Narcissistic

Manipulative

Devious

Vindictive

Security Point

Type Sixes may show positive, healthy levels of development in times when they are growing as opposed to Type Nine personalities.

These traits are considered healthy and include:

Independent

Self-sufficient

Patient

Self-effacing

Optimistic

The levels of development

Healthy:

Level 1

Self-affirming

High functioning Sixes display confidence that allows them to express themselves and inspires courage.

Niveau 2

Loving

They are easy to connect with others through their affection and love. They are able to build trust that can lead to relationships and alliances.

Level 3

Dedicated

They work hard for causes they believe. Their family and friends can count on Sixes to be there. They create an environment of safety and stability.

Average:

Level 4

Vigilant

They lose faith and trust in their opinions, and they look for reliable solutions elsewhere. They are always looking out for potential problems.

Level 5

Passive-aggressive

They might be indecisive and evasive in order to avoid taking on additional responsibilities. Many of these Sixes can be procrastinators.

Level 6

Sarcastic

In order to overcome their insecurity, they blame others. They take defensive measures and distinguish between friend versus foe.

Unhealthy:

Level 7

Panic-stricken

They panic when they feel unsafe or their plans fall apart.

Level 8

Persecuted

They can feel paranoid, and that everything is going to be against them. They can act out in a way that is self-fulfilling and destructive, especially in relationships.

Level 9

Hysterical

They look for escape routes from the life-shaming. They may seek out ways to escape the punishment of life. (Please contact a professional immediately if you or someone close to you is in this situation.

Chapter 12: The Enneagram & Religion

"The Enneagram isn't an original concept. However, typological personality types have been around since Nehemiah rebuilt the walls at Jerusalem."

-- Joe Carter

There haven't really been any disagreements with Christianity about the Enneagram. Many Christian circles and denominations still have differing opinions about the Enneagram. Some may have adopted the Enneagram for their spiritual counseling. But others just ignore it.

Although many argue that the Enneagram's origin is agonistic, there have been many Christians who have found immense value in the Enneagram. Although the Catholic Church has been extremely critical of it since its inception, many other Christians have taken to heart the personality typing.

It is important that we understand that Enneagram may not be the only tool used today in the body Christ. The Enneagram may be the most popular personality classification system, however, it was not the only one that was available in recent times. One of these is "The Four Temperamental Types of Hippocrates."

Joe Carter, Christian Analyst, Writer, and Editor stated, "While Enneagram may not be ancient, typological personality types have been around from the time Nehemiah rebuilds Jerusalem's walls." In fact, the four temperamental type developed by Hippocrates, an Ancient Greek Physician, were created between 460-397 BC.

His belief that certain human moods or emotional expressions are caused by body fluids, (humor), was based on known body fluids such as blood, black pile, yellow heap, and phlegm. Science has recently disproved the fact. The work of Plato (328-348 BC) further expanded the medical/temperamental theory. Galen later combined all four temperamental type into sanguine, melancholy (choleric), and phlegmatic along with the traits they entail.

Although many Christian organizations still use the four temperamental categories created by the Greek physician Hippocrates for their members, it is clear that the origin of this personality classification system wasn't "divine". Some schools of thought believe that it is essential to use the classifications systems, which were developed by philosophers as well as scholars, in light of Scripture.

What Christians Should Know about the Enneagram

The Enneagram, which has gained popularity in Christian circles over recent years, has seen a lot of use in the Christian world. Many priests have used the Enneagram to help them understand themselves more deeply, in the light God's Word. Many Christians use the Enneagram for marriage counseling to help them find compatible couples and teach them to embrace their weaknesses.

The Enneagram was a huge hit with younger evangelicals. Many Christians that have taken the test have written articles about its revealing and piercing powers and how they have benefited from it in their lives. Many Christians have written articles encouraging their fellow Christians to take these tests and then use the results for personal improvement in order to grow in their walk with God.

This has led a recent rise in popularity of Enneagram within Christian circles. What should Christians know regarding the Enneagram, however? What is the best way for Christians to use the Enneagram tool within the body of Christ's church?

A self-measuring/analysis tool.

The Christian body believes that only His World can help us to know ourselves in relation God. The World of God teaches nine character traits of God that should exist in His Children. They are: love; joy; peace; kindness; goodness. faithfulness. gentleness. self-control.

These traits are, in a sense the reflection of our "true divinity" which is something we should all strive for. If you look closely at the Enneagram, you will see nine strengths and six weaknesses for each personality trait. According to Enneagram Institute, if we can mask our weaknesses and reveal our strengths, we will be more successful. This may be true in hindsight. However, we should focus on developing the nine characters God uses the Enneagram method to spot weaknesses and strengths in our personalities.

After taking the Enneagram quiz, you can begin to analyze the nine character traits Paul spoke about in Galatians. Which of these "fruits," are most prevalent in your personal life? You might start to measure yourself using the Enneagram fruit scale.

Don't rely on Enneagram to develop your spirituality

The Enneagram should NOT be used for growth, but for personality discovery. As with all typing systems it will only provide some insights into your personality. You should not depend on the typing program for spiritual growth.

Deep relationships with God are the only way to true spiritual growth. You don't need to be discouraged by the Enneagram.

This is the moment to reach out to God for help.

It is important to realize that the Enneagram will not fix you. Only God has the power to save us. Although the Enneagram helps you determine where your weaknesses are, God is able to transform you by His grace through fellowship with Him. Trust God to help you grow and develop, not the Enneagram.

With a wider perspective, approach the Enneagram.

As humans, we love to understand and put things into context. God is a concern. But there might be more to the vices, and virtues, than what has been presented. A narrowing of your own actions or that of others can lead to confusion.

You should be open-minded and flexible when approaching the Enneagram. To see people through all of their lenses, you must learn to look at them from different perspectives. This will allow for you to understand the differences between people, and create a more loving relationship than focusing on one or two.

Emily Rise Massey a Christian journalist and author commented on the matter. Although it is beneficial to understand ourselves, that knowledge should not be limited to certain patterns, categories, or repeated behaviors. This is especially true if you are describing yourself within your Enneagram numbers. The cross of Christ is the ultimate source of our identity as believers.

COMPREHENSIVELY UNDERSTAND THE LIMITATIONS IMPORTANT TO THE ENNEAGRAM

Focus on how to work on yourself, and you will become a better version. This is how you can use your enneatype information to improve yourself. Keep your faith in God. He will show you more about your strengths, and less about your weaknesses. The Enneagram can be powerful, but it also has its limitations.

You don't have to rely on the Enneagram alone to figure out who you truly are. It is best to connect with your Maker to find out your strengths and weaknesses. God knows your identity better than any personality type. Christians need to be aware of this while they mess around with various Enneagram testing.

Guide to the Enneagram from a Christian Perspective

Many Christian faiths have recognized the effectiveness of Enneagram. It is essential that they view it from the right perspective in order to help people come closer to God.

The Christian church understands that sin is a result of the fall. We are born and bred in the sin. Sin is a part of every culture. Even when someone becomes a Christian their old ways are still deeply rooted within the subconscious mind. Christians were warned to "be transformed with the renewing mind."

Many of the problems people exhibit are their own fault. They have not made any effort to improve their own lives. The subconscious mind is still holding onto the weaknesses. The Enneagram helps you discover your "unconscious" thinking, feeling, and behavior pattern in order to self-correct them using the World of God.

How can you make improvements in your own life if you don't know where? To improve yourself, it is important to first understand yourself. Although the Enneagram does not have a Christian history, all tools and methods can be used in order to understand God's world. Prayfully use Enneagram, asking God to reveal your true self and help you understand it better.

It is crucial to recognize that the Gentiles had many ancient tools in their time to discover and understand themselves. Christianity didn't bring down self-discovery tools. Instead, it gave them a new way to use them. The Enneagram can be done in the same manner. Instead of being critical you should use Enneagram carefully and thoughtfully to identify your own deadly sins, and then return to God to receive healing.

You might also consider asking God to cleanse and purify your heart from all the uncleanness you have been unconsciously ingraining due to your personality. This will make Enneagram a lot more useful and valuable in your Christian walk. Paul mentioned that all are acceptable for Christians to use. But they are all useful and beneficial.

Thank God that the Enneagram can be used to benefit all religions. It should only be used in the light God's universe. At the end, you want God to work on you soul. Excusing yourself based on your personality type can also be wrong. You can't just excuse someone else for wrongdoing.

You must understand that wrongdoing can lead to serious consequences. The Bible warns us against sinful conduct and warns us that its wages can be death. You can be tempted to walk in pride. There will be a price. It is not worth being stubborn, slothful or lustful. Instead of making mistakes or condoning wrongdoing simply because of a personality type, it is better to walk in purity.

How to use Enneagram in order to improve your spiritual life

Ian Cron said "Insights is costly." He didn't believe insight could be used for anything other than the greater good of growth, transformation, and improvement. You are looking to increase your spiritual growth by using the Enneagram. You want to improve your life.

When working on yourself, your focus should be to seek God's help. It is vital that you always try to reach out to God for help in healing your soul and becoming the best version yourself. Dependence upon any other tool can be idolatry. If you are a Christian, it is important to not rely on anything but the finished work Christ has done to make you a better Christian.

It is essential to remember that it takes time for us to change our deeply rooted beliefs, behavior and way of living. It won't go away in a matter days. It takes patience and time in order to clean your subconscious mind. This is why it is so important to trust God.

The Enneagram may not be able to tell you if you are exhibiting or committing deadly sins. Type one might expect people to behave in a certain manner. He might be extremely critical of anything that doesn't look good or perfect. You may not understand the reason you display this self-righteous anger.

The Enneagram is a tool that will reveal this aspect of you personality. Once you are able to see your blind points, you can begin to think about how you can work on them. If you are married or in a relationship, it might be worthwhile to assess how your highly driven emotional drive is causing problems in your marriage.

Find ways to be more patient, understanding and kind with others. Look for ways to make people feel comfortable and understand their points of view. Do you find yourself criticizing your partner as much as you are?

If you are the type eight person who loves giving, you might want ta to pay attention to your hidden motives and how you give. Do you want to please people or is it for your own good? Is it to win others' approval? Is to gain the support of other people? Is it to become famous? Is it to make you famous? Is it to earn respect from others? Does it impress others?

While it is great to give, you should make sure you are doing so with pure motives. You could try the Enneagram as a way to get started in your "inner working". Begin to improve your self-esteem and stop allowing pride, arrogance, boastfulness, or an impressive motive to motivate you to give. Give cheerfully, without any pride. The Enneagram may be used in this manner to facilitate personal and spiritual transformation.

Chapter 13: Enneagram Super Heroes

The Enneagram consists of the nine basic types of personality traits and the higher fear-reactive attributes. Each one of us has some of the more prominent and important attributes among all nine forms. Reactive self: Inflexible, pliable. Argumentative, stubborn, cunning, cunning. Distracting, defensive. Moody. Sometimes it can be difficult to identify when we react to negative characteristics, even if our heart is in the right spot. A good way to observe this is to notice when you feel threatened.

Although superheroes may be seen as flawed, many people see them as good people who are trying to make the most from their situation. Our Enneagram Super Heroes (and their superego behavior) are available to help you visualize the deformities that can sometimes mask you.

Type ONE, ONEder Women - This extraordinary model of perfection is an exemplary model of perfection who can see the best in every situation. She is an exceptional example of perfection, making no mistakes and wanting everyone around her to be the same.

Yikes! Yikes! People make mistakes, standards are still relevant. It is not a good idea to insist that you do things in a certain way.

Form TWO, St Benevolence. The benevolent lady who is good and generous always gives and promises that everyone will be grateful. She never misses the chance to be rewarded in any way for her good deeds.

Real hospitality can be a reward all by itself and doesn't require any praise or acknowledgment. Perhaps you are looking for another motivator to share your good deeds with others, other than kindness.

Form THREE -- Captain Unbelievable -- This super hero never misses a chance celebrate his accomplishments and his possessions. His walls are lined by photos of important persons, and he rarely mentions his own name.

Excellence is your dedication, your work. If you think praise and recognition should be more important than the actual work, then consider why impressing other people is so important.

Form FOUR, The Dark Star — This superhero will battle through to the end against all odds. Unfortunately, she is also deeply misunderstood.

The higher self does no fight and should never be known. You may feel like a victim at any stage of your lives. If this is the case, then consider why your self-worth has been so heavily influenced by other people's approval.

Form FIVE Cerebrain -- This super-soldier knows almost everything about any thing in the world. Celebration knows everything but is not able to understand.

It's not necessary to impress anyone by your level of understanding. As long as you have faith in who you are and the things you know, there is no need to be a showman. Maybe it is time to reconsider why you are so uninformed when you display your intelligence.

Form SIX. Anti Hero - This superhero is capable of seeing everyone's suspicious motivations, criminal and otherwise. Anti-Hero cannot be trusted and so waits for action to bring them together.

It may be soothing for a short time to wait for things break down. But you can still say, "I knew it!" You can't wait for the worst, but it is almost certain to happen. Your true nature knows that all life is good and not so bad. This is a recognition of the times when things go well and the times when they don't.

Form SEVEEN: Adventure Man. Adventure Man has a thrill moment and never gets tired of fighting crime or saving damsels who are in trouble. This would slow him down. This enneahero is faster than anyone in the name if multi-tasking, which is a way to avoid accountability and avoid responsibility.

To avoid your emotions, and the confusion you create in others' lives, it is best to run your life at the speed that light. Your true nature does not rush to accomplish anything, because it knows it can do whatever it pleases.

Form EIGHT, Commander-Doubted. The Commander is a Commander-Doubted who has the ability to preserve peace and protect innocent civilians. He keeps track of every aspect in his life. His services are always available for God to watch over the world.

The authentic self can only know our thoughts and responds, which are controlled by us. It is a wasteful effort to regulate everything and everyone.

Type NINE. Amazing Disappearing Woman. The incredible disappearing woman pretends not to exist when arch villager's evil presence is revealed.

Because you know that your authentic self can handle any problems, you don't have to avoid them. It makes problems more difficult to hide.

What does the Study of Personality mean for you?

Personality is a narrative-like word. It's familiar and clear until it becomes hard to define. We find ourselves quickly lost in the maze if we try to generalize. We refer to personality types as a way of defining a person's personality. They also say that individuals have a distinct personality style. It is easy not to realize that it is impossible for a term to be described.

In fact, the reverse is true. Type of personality is a term which has been created because it has practical use. It's not about whether one can represent a person accurately using any style or personality theory. It is worthwhile to question why a good personality model is such a valuable tool in connecting with individuals. Just like stories, personality descriptions of good quality aren't true or false. We explain how and why we believe the truth.

A good personality system is able to help us remember that others may not think or respond the same as ourselves. This is an important reminder and a great way to help others. When we are trying influence others or interact with them, our instinctive tendency is to find common ground. Many people assume that shared motivations, beliefs and emotions are the same as ours. The principle behind personality allows us to see that everyone can choose different paths. The fact that we all have some commonalities does not mean we have the same ideas or values.

The second benefit is the ease of dealing with people. If we had to have an objective and fair view on everyone we have in our lives, we would have severely limited our interactions. There is too much information for a world where everyone is the result of unique combinations of experience and DNA. Personality theories make it possible to generalize and simplify, so we can come up with better solutions faster. It is not the facts; it is the best guess. However, it's more accurate than most people think. To quickly find the right direction in an interaction, or relationship, you can think of personality types and work hypotheses.

Researching personality theory can be a good idea for many other reasons. Understanding the various personality types will reduce stress in difficult relationships. Understanding motivation and behavior patterns can help you recognize the differences between relationships. Paradoxally, understanding personality can make these problems seem less serious. You will view your relationships differently, being curious about how misunderstandings occur and not just how they arise.

Psychologists, coaches and authors have also studied personality theories as they can help to create concrete strategies to improve the results of their work. Understanding how people adapt to changing environments and their beliefs is a benefit for everyone. Personality theories make it easier to discern patterns in seemingly inconsistent or random information about others. They make it easier to see what we can and cannot say or do.

Understanding the reasons we research personality provides us with parameters for testing various theories and structures. A program may be valid to support, but we don't need to make that judgment. It must be clear and systematic enough that it is easy to identify different types. Every reliable program should be considered a starting point. Comparing programs will help you find the one that best matches your communication needs.

The Enneagram (an Enneagram) is a model for personality types. It was created over many centuries and can still be used without paper examination. You might find it to be a good place to satisfy you curiosity and work with others.

The Enneagram, the Master Tool of Transformation

The Enneagram - an ancient device of unknown origin that some truly brilliant people claim was introduced to the world - is an ancient tool. Sufi numbers may also be referred as the chessboard or other wonderful development stuff.

The Enneagram displays the strengths as well as the weaknesses of every intelligent person born on planet Earth. This chart shows the nine basic personality types.

This is a modern interpretation of the nine forms personality.

1. The perfectionist is the top performer, a person who has a great deal discipline and strives for the best possible performance. They make very good villains, because they don't care what happens to human suffering.

2. The agent (or priest), also known to be the supporter. They are generally very service-oriented and love to support others. They often manipulate us into doing what they want. That is because it is the only right way to see the world. A theme can be described as a man who cries out to his God.

3. The chameleon has been called the climber. This handsome man is all good and beautiful, but his loveliness shows. You can watch them change as the crisis presents itself. Most people cannot believe that they are fake characters. They maintain a nice smile and good character outlook while actually separating themselves from their true emotions.

4. One who is sensitive to others' personalities can be a performer with personality. This leads to envy of what

others have done with the rest of their lives. Suicidal tendencies can be attributed to the fact that he is aware of his own needs and feels guilty. Others might think such a person exaggerates their emotional concerns.

5. The paranoid geek is paranoid. This man is smart, but also easily distracted. He sees logic connections in all things. He just wants the truth about the phenomena that is happening all around him. He might start to be paranoid and look for conspiracy theories or cure-alls. He loves to learn about his mind and wants to find a way that he can fit in with what he considers to be awful.

6. It is protected by devils. He could be a faithful steward or a bad sedative enemy-talker. He feels a lot of tension within him that he relies on to ease it. She believes that everyone is worse than the person he is loyal to. He may seem unconcerned and arrogant, but he's an extremely hard-working, masochistic guy.

7. The psychopath. The maniac. He's a peterpan, and he never grows. He's an always-failed boy. He screams and tries to get the things and stuff that are important to him that make his life difficult. It could be food or video games. He is greedy.

8. The dictatorship of the tyrant. He could also make a strong boss or dictator. He has a strong personality and is grounded in the end. He could act as a mafia chief when he feels unbalanced and threaten those who do not agree with him. He could be a hero, philanthropist and true hero.

9. The nine is world's most inconsolable person. An unconscious peace-builder who is constantly disconnected from the outside world. Sometimes they may be at your party with you, and then forget about you. Sometimes, they will have awakenings like this. But all the while, you were there!

In practice, Enneagram was used by trainers in group dynamics for transformation exercises that impact all parts of the human shadow weaknesses. With the ultimate goal of conquering them, It was an important subject of research that led to major breakthroughs for shadow master transformations.

Chapter 14: Empaths at Work

The unique challenges of being an empath in work can be different from other areas of your daily life. The fact that you have to make enough money to support yourself and your family is the main reason most people go to work every day is not negotiable. If you have children, the demand will be greater. Even if the company you own is self-employed, it will still be necessary to interact with others out of obligation to ensure you are earning a living and getting paid. The necessity to work in order to make a decent living may cause stress because you are unable or unwilling to deal with emotional or energetic overwhelm.

Understanding Your Unique Experiences

An empath is someone who can see the world differently than others. This can make it more stressful to work in a traditional workplace. The average workplace is stressful. There are many people who work in the same area, and they have to work together no matter how much they like each other. You can have people who are not compatible, people that don't get along, work that doesn't go as planned, blame others, or a stressful environment due to too many personalities. It is a lot like high school. Everyone is there because it is necessary and not because they wish to. This can lead many problems for everyone.

An empath will feel overwhelmed if there is stress, blame. a lack in interest in being there, anger, or aggression. It is possible to feel anxious or stressed just by being around the energy of others, even though you do not have any reasons. It is possible to feel resentful about your workplace or dread going into work every day because of the stress it causes. Even though you hate it, you have to go because you need to make a paycheck. This can add to your stress and overwhelm making it difficult to navigate the energy of your workplace.

Navigating Your Environment

You don't have to struggle to navigate your workplace. If you have the right tools and the right mindset, you can start navigating your workplace easily without feeling overwhelmed or anxiety. This simply means that you need to know what the environment will be like so that your energy, emotions, and behavior can adapt accordingly.

A good way to get a sense about how your workplace feels is to do so on a regular basis. The general energy that is present in the workplace should be constant, even if it fluctuates from time to time. Ask yourself what the top three characteristics of your workplace are when you think about it. Some people might describe the environment as "cheerful, friendly and overwhelming," while others may think it is "dark. dreadful. and angry".

Once you've gotten an overview of how your work environment feels, it is time to start looking at the reasons for the negative emotions and how they affect you every day. There may be a stressed boss, demanding customers, lazy colleagues, a hectic schedule or a low salary that make your job stressful. So that you can pinpoint where your unhappy energies and emotions are coming, you should highlight all of the reasons you dislike your workplace. Then think of ways that you can control these undesirable emotions and energies. For example, if your boss is stressful, or your customers can be rude to you, it might be worth shielding yourself against their energies and making sure your shield is always intact. If they do come into your space, you can reinforce your shield and affirm that no unwanted emotions or energies are entering your space.

To make things easier for yourself, take action to make positive changes in your life. Do not be afraid to voice your opinion and make a difference in your own life, even though it may seem difficult. Don't be afraid asking for a raise and promotion, seeking a different job, and asserting your boundaries so that your work is not overloaded. Speaking up for yourself reinforces the fact that it is not okay to be exploited and that your energy, emotions, and will must be respected. It will help you take control over your workplace experience and reduce stress levels.

Steps for dealing with others

There are several things you can do to make your workplace more enjoyable and help you stop feeling overwhelmed by work. Below are some ways you can make your work life more manageable.

Step 1: Assert and Set Your Boundaries

Your first step to making your workplace more effective is to establish and enforce boundaries. Because you may be fearful of what you will do if you establish boundaries, it can be hard for empaths to set them. If you have lived with narcissists in your life and have had to remove your boundaries, this may make it even more difficult.

Your personal space should be considered and a boundary set. Consider if you have to do all the work of your coworker, but your boss refuses to let you. You could tell your boss that you have stopped doing work that isn't yours, and ask your coworker to do the same. Your boss should know the true reason for your coworker not finishing work. You might feel uncomfortable and fear that you'll get in trouble. But, if they don't respect your boundaries, it will be possible to ensure that you're not being taken advantage or mistreated by your bosses and coworkers.

Step 2 Reinforce your Energetic Shields

If customers, coworkers and other office authorities come into your space with low energy or are unable to focus, reinforce your energy shield. Imagine a white energy ball moving through the energy field from your core, outwardly. It is okay to place a mirror at the end of it to help deflect their energy, and prevent them from reaching your personal energy fields. So you can avoid carrying around unwanted energy all day.

Step 3 Take Advantage of Your Holidays

It is important that you take time to rest and relax during your work breaks. To get away from the overpowering energies, take a walk outside of work for a couple minutes to relieve yourself. Even if you only have a few minutes to breathe in fresh air and ground your energies, it can make a big difference in helping you get rid of unwanted energies. Consider taking a short break to get some fresh air and running your hands through cold water. The cold water will wash away all negative energies.

Your Quick Start: Coping in your Workplace

Take the next step and identify the area in which stress is most severe. Then, use the following coping strategies to help you reduce stress. So that you feel safe in your workplace environment, start simple with grounding energy and strengthening your energetic shields. Start to notice areas in your work environment that aren't working and start to make positive changes. If you're unable to make immediate changes, set yourself up to be able to make them in the next few months. Sometimes it is enough to just have the hope that things will be different to help you relax.

Chapter 15: Enneagrams For Parents

Do you feel depressed when your child fails to behave in accordance with your expectations? Would you like your child to feel more confident? We often complain about children not following the path we choose. We try to force our children into following our wishes, even though we don't have the option of choosing their personalities. We have to learn how to work with them and let them know what to do. Are you trying to build a stronger foundation or change your behavior but don't know what?

The Enneagram consists of nine personality types that are used to describe the human condition. He recognizes the uniqueness of each person, but he can identify some common patterns in behavior. Realistically, we all have some elements of each of these nine types. One type will dominate, but we can learn to balance our differences and be more flexible.

You have to identify yourself with one of the nine types. However, you must also be attentive to the four types with the greatest connection: our wings & arrows. The position of the wings is on either side our enneagram. Many of the variations within each type are due to the inclinations towards the wings and the movements after the arrows. What are the different types of genotypes for children?

The Perfectionist Style

Enjoy all the food you have eaten and we'll be glad to help with the one dish.

He washes with his hands without protesting and takes a shower.

He does his homework and doesn't need to be reminded

He has a sharp-minded outlook: correct people's style of expression

Do your best to manage other children.

It will teach you better methods and reprimand your mistakes.

He is interested both in causes and ideals

He takes schoolwork seriously and criticizes those who don't.

UNO children strive to create an ideal world by being conscious, responsible, hardworking and caring. They are afraid of showing their vulnerability and anxiety because it seems others don't seem to care as much. These people are often angry because of this pressure. They are able to relax, have fun and explore the creative side of themselves.

The Auxiliary Fashion:

He often puts other peoples' wishes before his own, and it is rare for he to ask for what he wants.

You feel easily hurt by your feelings

He is drawn to people with problems and enjoys giving their advice.

He knows how to get people motivated to do what he wants.

He is more comfortable being with others than anything.

Show off your best features or look nice to draw attention

You should be a good student

He seems not to need any instruction, but he seems to know what the other wants or needs.

TWO people are always willing to help others. They are compassionate and will help those in need. They provide support and protection for their loved ones. They feel hurt and rejected when they have to deal with other people. They strive to get love and acceptance by helping others and acting well. They are not good at being kind and tell others what they want. It takes energy to please others. They could use that energy to discover and expand their own self-worth. They feel more at peace when they can think alone, engage in creative activity, and are more assertive and direct.

Style to Win

Do not give up until the end

It's easy to adapt to social settings

He likes to look clean, lustrous, and well-dressed

He's energetic and full of life, even though he's clearly tired of trying to do too much.

It has many skills.

He is efficient and quick.

He is most often optimistic and positive.

Winner-style children tend to be stressed out by competition, work, and always being first. Encourage him not to stress and make it a priority to relax for his health. Let him know he loves and appreciates him for who he truly is. Give him the opportunity to experience your emotions and encourage him into meaningful friendships. For the THREE, honesty remains the key. The problem with the THREE is that they are not able to claim what is truly theirs: their feelings, priorities and priorities. Your image is instead regarded as the most important. It is possible to help them overcome this trend by being respectful of their inner lives, helping with their concerns and encouraging their development of their principles.

Romantic Style

They feel pain easily

He wants to feel special

Want to have a closet filled with elegant clothes?

He is engaged in fantasy or absorbed games

It helps to make sense of the dramatic, both funny and tragic.

Enjoy the arts.

Think of things in a new and creative way

Sometimes it appears melancholic or depressing.

They may feel misunderstood. If your feelings are very intense, don't get so wrapped up in them. Instead, just be aware of what they are feeling. These children may need to step out of their comfort zone and get along with others to share their sense of humor and wit.

Style:

Can be either calm or timid.

He likes to be by himself and reads or does other things that interest his interests.

Is able to articulate clear opinions about most topics, but is also open to the interpretations of others

He is interested in understanding how things work as well as philosophical issues

He has an ingenious sense of humor

It is often found in the outermost part of the groups.

It appears you are not interested social norms

He is annoyed by the way people look at or pay too little attention to him.

The sensitive nervous systems and nervous system of the FIVE can be disturbed by loud or distressing sounds. They can use noise to manage their nerves if they have to. They will do anything to avoid discomfort. Some would prefer them to speak without having to think too much. A lot of people find one-on-1 contact more comfortable than being part of a group.

Interrogating Style

They are more concerned about safety then other children

Sometimes it responds in an extreme, contradictory and unpredictable manner

Change your mood often: nervous, restless or irritated.

He is averse to opposing the position of others.

He is anxious, suspicious, scared, and he may act out in an aggressive manner.

Try to please or entertain people

Rapid speech or stuttering

He has compassion to help those in need

Interrogator-style kids want to know the authority. They enjoy taking the initiative but are usually anxious about it. It is possible to help them trust their inner authority by being calm and firm in their ability for new situations.

Adventure Style

He is usually happy, and he gets up every morning to fall asleep.

Save any fascinating object you have discovered.

He loves to be the star

He loves meeting interesting people.

He has a contagious smile, and a smile that makes you smile

He has many friends

He is very curious and loves to know everything.

He enjoys telling stories, and laughing at jokes.

The ability to think in seven different ways is what children have. Even though they are often criticized for their inability to persevere, children can develop a vast knowledge base through experience and curiosity. Children can also possess many talents and can hold high ideals. It is important to see and appreciate their achievements and talents, as well as their appreciation for the world.

Assertive Style

Dominate other children

It has great energy.

Make your presence felt everywhere

He clearly displays his anger & dissatisfaction.

Teachers and kangaroos get a bad reputation for their stubbornness and stubbornness.

It revolutionizes everything and you have to stop.

Communicate and act with authority

Exercises in a joyful and enthusiastic manner

Eight children can be fiercely protective. They desire to feel the world in intensity. You might feel sad or hurt if you can't find energy to go on through amazing activities and nature experiences, or fun and activity, They won't hesitate to tell their parents what they think. Sometimes they will control their parents. They hate lies and hatred people. They can be aggressive and vindictive. Therefore, people fear not being able to agree with them. EIGHT children are often difficult to educate. These children will blame others and not take accountability for their actions. EIGHT children have a tender, warm and friendly side. They will respect you and trust you. It is important to be honest, direct, formal, sincere and respectful with them.

Pacifier Style

He likes TV, computer use, and bread baking at home9.

He loves to hug him and climbs onto his lap to hold his hand.

Reassure people by telling them that he is charming.

He has difficulty making decisions and is often a follower of others.

He says that everything is awesome, even though it might not be.

He talks and moves a little slower that most children.

He is very sensitive to the hurt feelings in his emotions.

It can be stubborn.

NINE children often feel a special connection to nature. Many others see them as less difficult to please than their own feelings. Treat the NINE like all children with compassion. Show them that your values them and that you can see and hear their needs.

By studying personality traits, it is possible to identify the type of personality that our children are. However, stereotypes are not without danger. You can react to someone and think it's a personality trait. The purpose of the Enneagram with children, is to allow them to accept and embrace different styles. It also helps to remind us that children transcend any type we assign to them. Do not try and assign types to people. Instead, make only hypotheses about yourself. While children do have predispositions, their behavior is constantly evolving and changing.

Chapter 16: How can you find inner peace and happiness?

Finding inner peace means that you can make peace with your past.

Step 1; Find strength and courage in solitude. Then, examine what you are lacking.

You can take each day off. Now, find a quiet spot and list all of the things you have been hurt by. You should not force your partner or self to think about everything if it doesn't come naturally to you. You can do this again and again if you need.

Writing down these details could be a difficult process that can take time to bear. You may end up crying the whole day. You might feel depressed. It is possible to not be as productive at the office. Be aware that your work may not be as productive. You do not have to force or endanger it. Allow yourself to dwell on the past.

As you begin to record everything in your past with honesty, you will have the ability to feel vulnerable again to the things that cause you pain. Once you do that, you will soon find the relief and happiness you want.

Step 2 -- Accept your past, however painful it may have been.

It is not doing anything if you refuse to accept the reality of your past. If you think things like, "I wish I weren't born to that family but did another," or "I wished my parents had more useful resources to improve my life," then you are only causing havoc.

It has taken me much longer and more effort to accept things as they currently are.

My childhood and growing up were so painful that I can't remember it well. First, I lost someone close and dear to myself when I was only six years of age. It's also something I keep in my mind that my mother did so much to make me happy and see me through. It is a constant reminder of these things that makes me feel weak. But I cannot let my past hurts define who I am. To make the best of my current circumstances, I remove my thoughts from those past events.

My whole world was shaken up when the fellow I spoke of died. We have been struggling to find our feet for many years and there are always reasons to mourn the loss. It was almost my entire life, but it did not define me.

But, I want to make it clear that once I was able to be myself, I stopped bringing the pain from my past into my future. I realized that the painful events in my past were real and I could see them for what they were. I realized that this helped me to relieve stress and became more relaxed. If you truly want to improve your life, then you will need to get to know yourself and use the enneagram of personality.

For years I was used to resisting what had happened before me. These things cannot be reversed or changed. Although it slowed down my development and progress I later realized this and made adjustments.

I am not going to speak for or convey the pain you feel from your childhood. I know that bringing those things to the surface can lead to extreme psychological effects and pain. If you continue to argue with what is happening, you are actually arguing against something that has already happened.

No matter how much effort or power and thoughts are put into it, the past cannot be changed. It will continue to remain the exact same. It is vital to find peace with the past. You must accept the past and make conscious decisions to move forward.

Repressing your past and accepting it is a way to find relief. This will stop your future from becoming endlessly difficult.

So, we can't help but accept it, no mater how terrible it was.

Step 3: Find good in every circumstance

All of our experiences contain a hidden gem. While it may be difficult to determine at first, once you learn to be friends with your past pain, you can begin to recognize the opportunities for positive and rewarding outcomes instead of only dwelling in the negative.

Ask yourself "What delicacies were triggered by my past traumatic experiences?" Maybe you found a way to become stronger. Maybe your past experiences have helped you to make a difference and help others. You wouldn't be the person you are today if your past events hadn't occurred.

My father's loss helped me develop self-trust muscles and lead me to discover ways to rely only on myself. I also sharpened my decision making abilities to the point where I fully believe in my capabilities. I always know that no matter the outcome, I can trust in myself. I became my own anchor.

Also, hardship can work in your favor. Writing down the things you are grateful for is a wonderful way to teach your mind how to be happy. Write down all the great things that you have learned from your past and make peace with it.

Step 4 Let go from the "should/shouldn't" notion.

To make peace and forget your past, you might try to change what happened. This strategy doesn't work.

The primary cause of our suffering is that we are prone to attach limiting beliefs back to our past. You can find limiting beliefs in different types, such as ought to have and shouldn't have. For example:

"My boss and my coworkers must have treated me with respect."

"My exhusband shouldn't have betrayed and stabbed me in my back,"

"My exwife should never have betrayed or stabbed"

Was it something that happened in your past? The only way to get the relief you want is to think that it "ought/ought".

This kind of thinking is only able to cause suffering when you say things such as "my father oughta have respected me". It should have occurred exactly as it actually did. You don't know why? Because it was just how it happened.

An excellent and practical method to reconcile your history with your current situation and circumstances would be this: "My dad behaved in a way that was due to the fact that his own pain, negativity, and damaging acquisition were killing him. He couldn't share them with anyone. It would be unimaginable, crazy, not practical, and even odd if he, despite all his troubles and what he faced, chose to treat me with respect. He did this by showing great regard and dignity.

It wouldn't have helped me. This is despite the fact that I said it a lot.

I discovered that what was causing me pain in my life was how I believed she ought to behave. Your perception of how things should have been could be a waste. It will not make things better or change the past. However, it can lead to feeling stuck in the present.

Step 5 (Don't try to get recognition and acknowledgement of the person inflicting pain on you).

Many people believe that they are searching for acceptance and recognition of those who have wronged them in the past. The pain and hurt of the past will alleviate your current pain. It will also help you to get rid of the hatred and hurtful emotions that still plague your life. You would expect that the offender will acknowledge their mistake, and then apologize. However, no matter what angle you take to verify the second heap, this can often be fatal.

Why would anyone want to make you feel guilty for the wrongs you did? You wouldn't want the person who poisoned that delicious platter of shrimp to come back and make sure you are still alive in the hospital. Would you like that? I'm certain you don't want it to happen.

This may be something you would like to hear from your parent. I made many mistakes and committed many blunders. I am aware of your pain, and I know you are truly hurt. I'm sorry. Even though you may want those words to be said, they might not be.

You might not be able to find closure with the person who wronged you. Consider asking yourself why you are so desperate for this from the other person.

Your emotions and healing process will not be helped by someone else's validation or acknowledgment. It's up to each person to establish peace and reconcile their past with their present and future. Social approval and validation won't get you to the place you want. You need to be aware of your personality type in order to use it to your advantage.

The self-harassment of the "I want you understand the hurt I caused you" belief is a limitation that will keep you from experiencing pain.

Realism is not your friend. You will be able patch up your past and not have to accept their acknowledgment.

Step 6: Forgive the people who hurt you.

You cannot start to find peace with your history until you forgive those who have hurt. Forgiving yourself is the best thing for you.

Assume that you are not being judgmental. I was there. You must remember, though, that you forgive only for yourself, and not for him/her or her.

Forgiveness may be the most difficult thing you can do. To be sincere in your forgiveness is an added bonus. You don't necessarily have to forge peace with your history. You will find these things beneficial to your growth. You will be able even to patch up with your mistakes.

Chapter 17: Prayers and Centers Of Gravity

It's fascinating to explore the links between prayer and enneagram.

Gurdjieff's Enneagram diagram was one of the many unanswered queries. It is the reason why the second conscious shock, which should have been between 8 and 9 or siand do instead, can be found between 5 - 7.

Gurdjieff explained at the time the enneagram was introduced and discussed shocks, that the wrong location was an indicator for the type of work required in order to deliver the shock.

For a more detailed explanation, we will need to look at the diagram from several different perspectives.

Divided by an arrow down the middle of the Enneagram, the two sides represent the upper stories and the lower stories respectively of man's energy centers, or chakras. (See diagram.) The diagram shows the lower story on the right side, and the upper story on the left. They are two triads. These subsystems are combined into one cohesive whole within a larger context. The main difference between the two stories is that the upper one represents a different level and working method than the lower. It could be summarized by saying the right side pertains to the physical centers and that of the astral centres.

Star of David, an incomplete Enneagram depicts the existence of the triads. It preserves some of this understanding by inverting an of the two triangles. This indicates its involutionary origin.

The traditional position of Christ at the right hand God Father assigns His Presence the LEFT side Enneagram. However, we must understand that this view is from the diagram itself and not from our perspective.

II. Centers of Gravity

Jeanne De Salzmann (and others) have often referred the "center for gravity" in man to mean that there is only one center of gravity. However, this isn't the exact case.

The dominant center in gravity for the lower level story is at position 4. This represents the lower half of the central nervous plexus. It is located in center of the lower torso. This lower portion of plexus is located under the navel.

The upper story's center gravitational point is in position 5, commonly known as the sunplexus. This is the Chakra center, and it occupies the heart position.

Zen, Tai Chi Qigong and Zen are some of the Eastern esoteric traditions. They all emphasize the center for gravity and all the other centers in the lower portion (or nervous system) of the body.

This practice does not clarify that while it can provide great power if utilized fully, it only answers half of the question. We are not surprised to see it associated with magic or healing powers as well as martial arts. Dogen's contempt for these homegrown traditions, which seem to be being assimilated into mainstream Buddhism as well as other esoteric practices, might have been due to his superior understanding.

In reality, we only have a limited understanding of how the energy system works.

This information can be clearly seen in the Enneagram, which simply shows it visually. On either side of this diagram, you will see that the Enneagram has both 4 (abdomen), 5 (heart) and 2 (heart). Once one has seen it, the information becomes clear.

Gurdjieff calls the first conscious shock the process of working on the lower stories. This shock, at position 3, is known as "conscious work." This is a discipline which is directly related to Hatha Yoga. Logically speaking, the first stage is physical yoga. It has an impact on both the triad that it belongs to as well as the entire diagram.

Gurdjieff taught us that working on the higher story (that is, the left part of the diagram) is possible through the second conscious trauma, associated with intentional suffer.

167

The first step in inner effort is opening the emotional centre. The reason the second conscious shocked is placed next the heart is to indicate that the first stage of work involves the opening and maintaining the heart.

Paradoxally this must happen long before the required energy for the passage between 8 and 9, or sito, arrives. The center of gravity can be found in the opening of your heart. It is used to cause intentional suffering and complete the left side. The geometry of the Enneagram contains an illustration of the mysterious parable: "To he that has shall much receive."

It may be of interest to readers to contemplate the essences of the first shock, which can be egoistic or involutionary, as well as the second shock, which can be compassionate and evolutionary. These two characters easily integrate with other understandings of the Gurdjieff method.

III. III.

It is apparent that Gurdjieff began working with an intellectual influence. He was influenced by the Yogi (or, as it is more commonly known, Djana Yoga). He told his proteges, "A man who completes this work would know the steps necessary to complete the Work of Bhakti and Hatha Yoga (that is, the Way of the Monk/the Way of the Fakir). Gurdjieff would have been well aware that he had completed the Way of the Yogi when he first met Ouspensky. Along with the intimidating and overwhelming amount of theoretical information he shared to his students he taught many Hatha Yoga techniques in secret.

Yet, his work grew more compassionate and emotional over time. He also began to de-emphasize some other practical work (especially intellectual theories). It seems clear (to me at least) how he realized that it was impossible to finish the Enneagram project without the full participation and support of the emotional center.

That is, Gurdjieff reached the end of his journey by choosing the path that was Love.

We can therefore say with some certainty that the man actually embodied a fully realized incarnation which combined all three paths. The culmination was however firmly grounded within Love. The unusually strong affinity between Gurdjieff Work Christianity and Sufism is a result.

IV. Harmonious Development

The Enneagram has no linear development progression. Instead, it is a dynamic system with a number of numbers from 1-9. The system contains all of the notes. This is because all of them exist, which is what is actually true in man's physical reality. All that is needed is to connect and build right relationships with them.

Therefore, the idea that one should be focused on only one part of a diagram is incorrect. This is why works can fall, if they do, by presuming that the main goal of work involves the concentration and control of power in the abdomen.

The Enneagram helps to show that there is more to the development question. All of the notes should be worked on simultaneously. This is subtle and does not allow for manipulation. It is a gentle, slow-paced process that can last for many years. All other techniques may produce amazing results, but they are more likely to lead to lopsided results.

Gurdjieff was well-versed in the inner energie system, and presented a work that was perfectly balanced. The Enneagram gives you a simple way to get to the bottom of these relationships.

V. Two Prayers

Gurdjieff works only has two principal prayers. This may seem odd for a religious practice, especially an esoteric Christian. We don't need to feel that this is unusual. The early Hesychasts were able to reduce their practice to one prayer. It was the "Lord give Mercy" prayer. They believed it was sufficient to obtain salvation.

While this could be debated, it is clear that Gurdjieff made sure that only the most important prayers were included in his system.

This is because each Prayer is specifically related with one side of Enneagram.

VI. VI.

This prayer refers to the Abrahamic prayers, which are the Old Testament prayers for Being that paved the way for Christianity. It comes from the statement Moses made by the Lord to Moses in the burning bush when he encountered him: "I Am that I Am."

This prayer is specifically about the first conscious surprise, conscious work, which is a work that affirms. This particular work deals with the energy on right side (yoga, the "rightchannel" or "golden strand," which runs down from right temple to bottom . This energy, esoterically referring to individual work and their personal effort, is directly linked to the individual. This work could be understood as an attempt to make oneself worthy through preparation. However, there are many dimensions to it.

VII. VII.

This prayer represents the Christian prayer. It is also the Prayer of the Heart. As practiced in the Early Church Fathers of the Philokalia, it is also the Prayer of the Heart. It is part of the Enneagram's left side, the second conscious surprise. This work concerns the energy in the left channel (yoga's left channel), that is sent to the body by God the Father (the Right Hand). The prayer is a call out for help. This practice is fundamental in Islam as well as Christianity.

Both prayers must be said in order to encourage harmonious development.

Because each one of them is associated specifically with a conscious trauma, we can see that worship in both Old and New Testament is an essential component of Gurdjieff. It's just worship in an unfamiliar environment.

This makes sense because, if you want to discover a new and effective worship, it won't necessarily be one you're already familiar with.

VIII. More about the prayers

Both the prayer and the two conscious shocks take on the roles of both holy affirming as well as holy denying. This relationship can be complicated but it is important to try to understand.

I am what you want me to be

The first shock, conscious labor is accompanied by a prayer to affirm the self.

This is natural because it happens on the right enneagram side, which is the corporeal or incarnated side. This is identical to Gurdjieff's statement that a man has to become a conscious, or incarnated, egoist to work. Embodied in flesh, the first task for a human being to do is to assert themselves consciously. This is how one takes responsibility for his or her Being.

This is a holy denying, because one must

In paradox, one can deny the Lord to affirm oneself. It is noteworthy that Gurdjieff was the mythological protagonist Beelzebub who fell from grace at heaven due to his assertion of himself and other ideas, rather than His Endlessness. We can see the direct connection between Beelzebub's actions as well as the explanation of why his exile--that is to be incarnated in the solarsystem--is evident.

The Beelzebub is in everyone.

The energy of the first conscious shock is involutionary. See Beelzebub's Tales To His Grandson (1040-1046). It is a folding backward of the higher toward the self, and a regathering decentralized energies (see Novel. Myth. & Comsos). This shock is affirming in the self's view, but denial in the Lord's. It is necessary for the entire process. One might think that to come back to the Lord, one must first leave Him. The parable concerning the prodigal boy comes to mind.

This understanding also sheds light to the notion of original crime in Christianity. Man must start from a point of holy denying (affirmation or denial of one's self), which is required for his existence. It is not an option. This view is in agreement with Meister Eckhart's thoughts on sin's nature. Brother Lawrence stated that he had placed his sins among God and himself, in order to warn God that it was not worth him. God continued to send blessings despite his indiscretion. (See The Presence of God: The Practice of His Presence.

The path is fraught by danger because it must be. (Job 5.7: But man is born to trouble, just like sparks fly upward. No one is exempted from having to negotiate this territory. The distinction between the conscious and unconscious self-deprecating egoists comes down to the fact that the conscious egoist is alert to the danger while the unconscious egoist ignores it.

One important esoteric purpose of the first prayers is to defeat the fear within oneself. This point of work can be both extensive and personal. Jeanne De Salzmann once said that we desire not to become--that is, we turn away form who we are. This turning away is caused by a deep fear that must be confronted to enable "Real I", Gurdjieff referred to as, to manifest.

All praise be to the Lord.

Intentional pain is the second conscious shock. It requires a move to the spiritual and emotional sides of the enneagram.

This shock is completely opposite to the original shock. This is a holy affirming step, a surrender to God. It's the surrendering of your ego that was so painstakingly, actively, affirmed in stage one of work. The holy denying of the ego, called shock, is what shock is.

This shock is the breaking of the heart. Chartres' maze symbolizes the path to your heart. Its center lies horizontally at the same distance from the church entrance as the image depicting Jesus at its center in the West Rose Window.

Finality will require us to let go of everything we have. The second shock, which is evolutionary in nature, involves a turning away from everything that was folded inwardly in the previous stage. Like organic molecules need to be correctly folded so they can do their jobs, the second shock must be correctly unfolded.

What is the secret to this system? Gurdjieff, in conversation with Ouspensky gave us an indirect answer. He said that men have already decided that they would get it and do not make an effort to achieve it.

It is impossible, if not in the same spirit to surrender one's self to God.

Gurdjieff stated that what we consider ego, or "I," actually is false personality--a constructed of the intellectual brain. (See Gurdjieff Views From The Real World.143; Ouspensky In Search Of The Miraculous.226-227. To have something to give up, or offer, you need to work hard.

These shocks can be multi-dimensional. Each shock can embody both a "yes" and "no". The shocks have an internal friction that keeps it moving. The beauty in understanding the system through this perspective is that there is always a reconciling factor, no matter how the shocks play.

In order to reconcile all our contradictions, it is necessary for the Lord to take action.

Conclusion

This book explains the Enneagram in detail. The ability to read personalities can improve your relationships. It will help you interact with people better and be more comfortable around them. It is easier to be able and to relate to others. This will make you feel more fulfilled. Also, you were provided with information about your Enneagram Type. This provides valuable information.

If you haven't taken an Enneagram, this is the next step. You will then be able apply the knowledge that you have gained. If you're looking to strengthen your relationship with someone you love, encourage them to take the test along. They can then look at their Enneagram pages to learn how you can best serve them. You will be able to start to analyze and correct any weaknesses in your behavior.

I want to thank you again for buying this book and learning all about your Enneagram types within it. Leave an

Amazon review if the book provided you with useful information. Your input and opinions would be greatly valued and will provide invaluable insight as to what was done well, and what needs improvement. I am grateful and wish you every success in your journey.